SCUBA DIVING INDUSTRY MARKET SIZE RESEARCH REPORT

(2ND EDITION)

SCUBA DIVING INDUSTRY MARKET SIZE RESEARCH REPORT

(2ND EDITION)

WORLDWIDE SALES OF DIVE GEAR, SCUBA DIVING CERTIFICATIONS, DIVE TRAVEL & DIVE SHOP SERVICES

DARCY KIERAN

WWW.BUSINESSOFDIVING.COM

Copyright © 2024 Darcy Kieran. All rights reserved.

www.businessofdiving.com

Cover photo: Shutterstock.

MODELS: Individuals in all pictures including the cover are models and used for illustrative purposes only. They are not related to the author or the publisher.

COPYRIGHT: The purpose of copyright is to encourage authors to produce works that enrich our culture and society. Uploading or distributing any content from this book without prior authorization is theft of the author's intellectual property. Please respect the author's work as you would your own.

For permission requests, course adoptions, quantity sales, and special orders, please email: publisher@businessofdiving.com

SCUBA DIVING INDUSTRY MARKET SIZE RESEARCH REPORT (2ND EDITION): WORLDWIDE SALES OF DIVE GEAR, SCUBA DIVING CERTIFICATIONS, DIVE TRAVEL & DIVE SHOP SERVICES

ISBN: 978-1-7390198-2-2 (color, paperback)

v 2.2

*To all my friends and colleagues
who have tolerated and participated
in my endless discussions on the size of the dive industry!*

*Next, we still have to discuss
a new business model
for a dive industry adapted to today's consumers!*

Contents

Section 1: Setting The Stage

1: What Is The Goal of This Book? 1

2: What Do You Mean by "The Size" of The Dive Industry? 3

3: Challenges & Limitations in Measuring the Size of The Dive Industry 4
    Dive Gear 4
    Dive Training 7
    Dive Travel 9
    Dive Industry Expenses vs. GDP 9

4: Warning: An Epidemy of Fake Market Data Studies 10

Section 2: Reviewed Market Data & Statistics

5: BEA – Bureau of Economic Analysis 17
    Water Activities' Products & Services 17
    Outdoor Recreation Trips & Travel 19
    Value-Added Outdoor Recreation by State 22

6: SFIA: Sport & Fitness Industry Association 24
    Water Sports Participation 25
    Scuba Diving Participation 26
    Snorkeling Participation 28
    Swimming Participation 30

Stand-Up Paddling Participation 31
Surfing Participation 32
Golf Participation 33
Dive Gear Manufacturers' Sales 34
Socio-demographic Profile of Scuba Divers 35
Scuba Diving Participation Rate by Age Groups 35
Scuba Diving Participation Rate by Race 35
Scuba Diving Participation Rate by Gender 36
Other Scuba Diving Demographics 36

7: OIA: Outdoor Industry Association 36

8: Dive Center Business Magazine 37
Number of Dive Centers in the USA 37
Impact of The COVID-19 Pandemic 38

9: Leisure Trends 38
Dive Gear Retail Sales 39
Total Dive Retail Sales 39
Average Revenues per Dive Center 40
Split of Revenues by Categories in Local Dive Shops 40
Split of Dive Gear Revenues by Type 41
Dive Training Statistics 42

10: U.S. Census Bureau 43
Dive Regulator Imports 43
Dive Regulator Exports 44

11: Dive Gear Manufacturers & Brands 45
Scubapro (Johnson Outdoors) 46

    Mares & SSI 46

    Beuchat 49

    Aqua Lung 49

    Brownie's Marine Group 50

    Decathlon 50

    Dive Gear Manufacturers Wrap-Up 50

12: RSTC Europe 51

13: TIV Tauchsport Industrieverband – Germany 52

    Dive Gear Sales – Germany 52

    Dive Gear Sales – Europe 53

    Split of Dive Gear Revenues by Type 53

    Entry-Level Certifications 54

    Participation 54

    Gear Expenses by Diver & New Diver in Germany 55

    Training Expenses per Diver in Germany 56

    Travel Expenses per Diver in Germany 56

14: DEMA Diving Equipment & Marketing Association 57

    Dive Gear Sales 57

    Split of Gear Revenues 58

    Entry-level Certifications in The USA 59

    Entry-Level Open Water Certifications by State 59

    Certification Per Capita by State 63

    More Data Points: USA / California / Florida 66

15: PADI Professional Association of Diving Instructors 68

    Retail Sales – USA 69

    Retail Sales – Outside the USA 69

Number of Dive Centers – Worldwide 69

16: Centre for Conservation Geography – Australia 70

17: Rebreather Forum 71
Rebreather Diving Certifications 71
Rebreather Diving Certifications by Geographic Market 72
Rebreather Units Sold 72

Section 3: Business of Diving Institute Surveys & Studies

18: Scuba Try-outs / Discover Scuba Diving 73
The Dropout Rate 73
Number of Scuba Tryouts in The World 74
The Size of The Scuba Tryout Market 74

19: How Much Scuba Divers Spend Annually on Dive Gear, Travel, Training & Services 75
How Much Scuba Divers Spend Annually on Training 77
Percentage of Scuba Courses Done Locally 78
How Much Scuba Divers Spend Annually on Dive Gear 78
How Much Scuba Divers Spend Annually on Used Dive Gear 78
Where Scuba Divers Buy Their Dive Gear 79
Split of Dive Gear Purchases by Category of Product 79
How Much Rebreather Divers Spend Annually on Rebreathers & Rebreather Supplies 81
How Much Scuba Divers Spend Annually on Renting Dive Gear 81
How Much Scuba Divers Spend Annually on Servicing Their Dive Gear 81
How Much Scuba Divers Spend Annually on Cylinder Fills 81
How Much Scuba Divers Spend Annually on Dive Outings & Dive Travel 82

Scuba Divers Who Also Participate in Freediving & Snorkeling 82

20: DIVE GEAR MANUFACTURERS SALES CHANNELS
    & ONLINE SALES 83

21: BENCHMARKING LOCAL DIVE SHOPS IN WESTERN EUROPE
    & USA 84
    Number of Employees per Scuba Diving Center 84
    Number of Divemaster & Dive Instructors per Scuba Diving Center 85
    Percentage of Dive Center Revenues by Department 85
    Average Sales of Dive Gear per New Student-Diver 86
    Product-Mix in Local Dive Shops 86

22: BENCHMARKING DIVE RESORTS 88
    Products & Services Offered in Dive Resorts 88
    Percentage of Dive Resorts' Bookings by Sales Channel 89
    Commissions Paid by Dive Resorts 89
    Number of Employees per Dive Resort 90
    Number of Divemaster & Dive Instructors per Dive Resort 90

23: THE SIZE OF THE DIVE INDUSTRY 90

SECTION 4: WHAT'S NEXT?

24: HOW TO ACCURATELY MEASURE THE SIZE OF THE DIVE
    INDUSTRY 93

ALSO FROM DARCY KIERAN 96

FEEDBACK, PLEASE 101

CONNECT WITH US 101

About Us 101
    About The Business of Diving Institute 101
    About Darcy Kieran 102

Section I: Setting The Stage

1: What Is The Goal of This Book?

There are several reasons why you may want scuba diving industry statistics and market data. You may be preparing a business plan for a new dive company or want to grow your current dive business. Perhaps you want to leave your boring full-time job in a soul-crushing cubicle and "dive in." But can you make a living out of it?

Dive industry market data is vital to managing your scuba diving business professionally. It can help you decide whether to buy or sell a business in this industry, which target market you want to go after, what marketing message you want to use, and more. Scuba diving industry statistics are valuable for every business decision you have to make.

Unfortunately, when you try to analyze the dive industry, the first thing you notice is a severe lack of dive industry market data and low reliability of the statistics you actually find.

Let's imagine that running a business is like sailing. It can be challenging to bring the yacht to port in a storm while being blindfolded with no GPS. You get the picture! And that is precisely what it is like to manage a business without data. Welcome to the dive industry!

In all other sectors I've worked in, we had readily available market and financial data on the industry, including market trends. However, once I bought my first dive business, I was facing a significant lack of market information. I bought it out of passion but without any market data to even try to pretend it was a rational decision. My accountant was not impressed!

Since then, through the Business of Diving Institute, we've conducted numerous dive industry market surveys and studies to help dive professionals like you and me.

In this book, we will summarize our findings, but first, we will examine other sources of dive industry data to put things in perspective.

Some statistics are publicly available, but most dive industry financial and market information is hidden.

Part of the reason we are all blindfolded is that we do not have a proactive dive industry association. For instance, in the USA, it is mind-boggling that we get more valuable statistics about scuba diving from the SFIA than from DEMA. DEMA is our Dive Equipment and Marketing Association. SFIA is the Sports and Fitness Industry Association. Let that sink in for a minute. We get more scuba diving industry data from the *fitness* industry association than from the *dive* industry trade association!

There are many reasons why DEMA is not collecting and providing the data a typical trade association would, but that discussion goes beyond the scope of this book.

So, we did an extensive search to identify available market and economic data sources on the scuba diving industry. We studied them to determine which ones were reliable. Then, we summarized data points collected from these sources and analyzed them to measure the sector, including the size of the scuba diving equipment market, dive training, and dive travel. It is like a gigantic 3D math puzzle!

In addition to our numerous Business of Diving Institute surveys and market studies, we reviewed data from multiple sources, including OIA, BEA, DEMA, SFIA, U.S. Census Bureau, TIV Germany, RSTC Europe, Scubapro, Mares, SSI, Beuchat, Aqua Lung, BWMG, Shearwater, and PADI.

Although we have reviewed data sources from around the world and used them to evaluate the worldwide size of the dive industry, we have more data from the USA and Europe than from other places. If you know of sources of dive industry market data that we have not reviewed in this book, please kindly let us know at businessofdiving.com/contact so that we can help more dive professionals.

Furthermore, we continuously run dive industry surveys and market studies. We need your help to increase the participation of dive professionals worldwide. Let's start right now! Please go to businessofdiving.com/help to take part in the surveys we are currently conducting. Your participation in these surveys will contribute to a better understanding of the dive industry, which will benefit all dive professionals.

At the end of this book, in a discussion about "What's Next," we will establish a methodology we could use as an industry to accurately and finally be able to measure the size of the dive industry in various markets and define trends.

For now, summaries presented in this book are the most official unofficial numbers for the scuba diving industry market.

2: What Do You Mean by "The Size" of The Dive Industry?

Scuba diving is a luxury, and as such, it is about emotions, not transactions. People do not leave their couches at home because they dream of buying dive gear! They seek adventure or a connection with nature—or something like that.

However, to measure the size of the dive industry, we want to look at transactions. As a dive store owner, I couldn't deposit 'great emotions' into my bank account, nor could I use them to pay the staff.

So, what transactional items are we giving to customers in exchange for their cash? It is actually not an easy question to answer.

In most industries, collecting market data is a straightforward process. For instance, the clothing industry has manufacturers, distributors, and retailers, but they all sell a specific product type—a physical product.

In the dive industry, nothing is forthright. It is one of the most complex industries to analyze because a typical dive center is really a mix of six sectors in one:

- **Gear Sales**: From manufacturers to consumers via brands, distributors, and retailers.
- **Training** is a whole different type of business. In our case, it involves a bunch of small, specialized schools, and on top of that, there is a group of independent instructors frequently paid under the table.

- **Travel** is yet another entirely different industry. And which part of travel are we talking about anyway? The business of being a travel agent is quite different from the business of operating a dive resort for tourists.
- **Repair & Maintenance**: This part is like managing a garage, and relevant metrics differ from those of a retail store operation.
- **Renting Gear** is an enterprise like Avis car rental. You own a pile of assets that you try to utilize.
- **Fill Station**: That one is like a gas station.

So, when you ask about *the size of the dive industry*, what exactly do you want to know?

For instance, if you include travel in the size of the dive industry, then gear and training will be tiny parts of a multi-billion dollar travel industry. But if you are a dive gear manufacturer and planning sales targets for next year, that big number would be useless.

Each of these six sectors has a different set of management metrics. And each of these categories of products and services has specific challenges associated with collecting data, which we will discuss next.

3: Challenges & Limitations in Measuring the Size of The Dive Industry

Measuring the size of each one of the six sectors part of the overall dive industry comes with its own set of unique challenges.

Dive Gear

If you are preparing a business plan for a dive store, you are mainly interested in how much dive gear is sold through dive stores. Typically, it means recreational scuba and snorkeling equipment. But if you are a dive gear manufacturer, the "size of the market" includes military sales, which for some manufacturers can be half their sales.

In this book, we look at the recreational scuba diving industry because military and commercial diving are two totally different beasts. In the

3: CHALLENGES & LIMITATIONS IN MEASURING THE SIZE OF THE DIVE INDUSTRY

rest of this book, "the dive industry" means the recreational scuba diving industry.

To be clear, though, "recreational diving" includes tech diving, which is an advanced form of recreational diving.

Otherwise, when discussing the dive gear market, we talk about "dive gear manufacturers" because that is how they are referred to in the jargon of the diving industry. But to understand the sector, you have to realize that many of these so-called manufacturers are really just marketing brands. Most wetsuits, for instance, come from a handful of Asian suppliers. None of the "dive gear manufacturers" selling scuba diving wetsuits actually manufacture wetsuits. The same applies to masks, snorkels, and many other dive gear items.

So, what gear should we include when evaluating the size of the dive industry?

Selling snorkeling gear is usually a big part of dive store sales and is definitively a significant component of the sales of dive gear brands. After all, there are about three times more active snorkelers than scuba divers in the world.

But even if we typically assume that snorkeling gear is included in dive gear sales numbers, how could we capture all snorkeling gear sales when evaluating the size of the market?

First of all, should low-end snorkeling gear sold by dive gear brands to large retailers like Costco and Walmart be included in our numbers? Some of that equipment can barely be used for more than fooling around in the backyard pool for half a summer! On the other hand, snorkeling gear sold in dive shops tends to be more high-end equipment. Should all of it still be part of our evaluation of the size of the dive industry? If we survey dive gear manufacturers' sales of fins, masks, and snorkels, these sales numbers are included.

Besides, how could you know for sure if the end-user buying a set of fins is a snorkeler or scuba diver?

In parallel to that, big retailers often source gear independently for their in-house brands, as Decathlon does in Europe. Their dive and snorkeling gear sales numbers are usually not part of a survey of dive gear sales conducted with dive gear manufacturers. And we shouldn't underestimate the snorkeling and diving revenues from these in-house brands. Let's not forget that Decathlon brought the highly successful full-face snorkeling mask to market.

A retailer may order its in-house brand BCDs from a known dive gear manufacturer. In that case, if we evaluate the size of the industry by looking at dive gear manufacturers' revenues, these BCDs are included. But if the same retailer orders masks directly from a Chinese supplier, these numbers bypass a survey of traditional dive gear manufacturers.

This leads us to another problem – a structural challenge with the way we collect data. Because it is hard to survey manufacturers, dive gear sales are often evaluated by multiplying the number of dive stores in a market by the average sales of a dive shop. But that leaves a big part of the market out, namely sales of dive gear in other retailers like West Marine in the USA and online dive gear retailers that do not operate a traditional dive shop.

And even within dive store sales, what should we include or exclude? Spearfishing and freediving gear? Probably yes. A lot of it is sold by dive gear manufacturers and dive stores. But dive stores sell all kinds of other stuff!

For instance, the Business of Diving Institute conducted a study on dive store average revenues. But how much of that top-line is actually from dive gear? And how much of it is from T-shirts and apparel sales? There is no limit to what dive store owners may decide to sell in their stores. Some dive stores sell surfboards! So, you must dig further to sort out what part of it is from dive gear.

And, wait! That's not all! What about Apple watches? The Apple Watch Ultra can be used as a scuba diving computer, so if somebody buys one instead of a traditional dive computer, the amount spent on that Apple watch is squarely in the dive industry. But most people use an Apple watch for more than one purpose. Even if we know how many Ultra were sold by Apple, it doesn't tell us how many were sold to people who intend on using it as a dive computer.

3: CHALLENGES & LIMITATIONS IN MEASURING THE SIZE OF THE DIVE INDUSTRY

So, as we said earlier, it's a gigantic 3D puzzle – maybe 6D!

In this book, we will try to make sense of it all.

DIVE TRAINING

A metric often used to evaluate trends in the dive industry is the number of entry-level open-water certifications.

It used to be reasonably easy to find that kind of information, especially when the dive training agency with the largest market share, PADI, reported its annual number of certifications. But once PADI no longer had a high rate of growth, they stopped reporting! And since then, their market shares have shrunk, so the information wouldn't be as representative as it used to be.

We can get bits and pieces of data on the number of certifications here and there. For instance, in the USA, DEMA produces a quarterly report on the number of entry-level certifications. But only three dive training agencies contribute to the report!

Otherwise, knowing how many new divers got an open water certification does not tell us the size of the dive training market in dollars (or any currency) because dive centers and instructors make the sales to consumers. Therefore, the training agency issuing the C-card does not know the price of the course.

And all of this is about entry-level courses.

Traditionally, the dive industry's business model has been highly tied to training new divers—selling them entry-level courses, a complete gear set, and sending them on their first dive trip. But that is a dying business model for many reasons that go beyond the scope of this book. If you are interested, join the business model conversation at www.businessofdiving.com.

However, regardless of the business model, dive instructors and centers earn revenues from diving training beyond the entry-level. For instance, in recent years, we noticed that the tech diving training market was healthier than the entry-level market.

Another way of estimating the market is to survey dive centers to establish an average level of training revenues and multiply it by the number of dive centers in the market. However, that method misses all revenues generated by independent instructors. Furthermore, dive training agencies have now started bypassing their own "members" by selling directly to consumers. And dive training agencies are famous for being secretive.

Even if dive training agencies were to stop being paranoid and contribute to establishing dive industry metrics that would benefit everybody, including themselves, we would still have the issue of double counting. It rarely happens at the entry level but is often seen at more advanced levels of training. For instance, a diver may take a course and get two certification cards for equivalent levels from two different training agencies. And if our goal is only to count the number of active divers, then the double-counting becomes even more significant. For instance, in the same year, a diver may get an advanced certification from dive training agency A and a rescue diver certification from dive training agency B.

In the past, some dive training organizations have made efforts to use a third party to review data and eliminate double counting. This was done for the Rebreather Forum, for instance. However, that process requires training agencies to provide databases with a way to identify individuals. And recent laws on privacy make such endeavors almost impossible to accomplish legally.

Otherwise, should scuba tryouts like "Discover Scuba Diving" be included in the size of the dive industry? We think so. It is squarely part of dive business operations, especially in tourist destinations. However, in many cases, dive operators perform scuba tryouts and discover scuba diving experiences without reporting them to a dive training agency. In fact, as we will see in this book, the number of unreported scuba tryouts is several times bigger than the official number for reported ones.

Finally, there's another significant issue with evaluating the size of a regional market because scuba diving is highly tied to travel.

So, for instance, many Canadian scuba divers have never dove or visited a dive center in Canada. They may have taken their certification course in Bonaire and bought their dive gear in Florida. Tourist destinations like

3: CHALLENGES & LIMITATIONS IN MEASURING THE SIZE OF THE DIVE INDUSTRY

Thailand issue many scuba diving certifications to tourists from around the world—Europeans, North Americans, Chinese, and the list goes on.

The number of active scuba divers in a specific market does not indicate the number of potential clients in that market.

For instance, the SFIA provides a reasonably reliable number of Americans who are active scuba divers in the USA. However, that survey does not tell us how many of them spend dollars in the USA. And vice versa, maybe scuba divers in the Florida Keys come from outside the USA.

As we said earlier, it's a giant puzzle! We'll try to make some sense of it for you.

DIVE TRAVEL

Here comes another set of challenges!

What should we include in the cost of a dive trip?

Let's say you are going to the Galapagos for an entire week of intense scuba diving and do not intend to participate in any other activity. In that case, the cost of the whole trip, including airfare and lodging, could be considered expenses spent directly in the dive industry.

But what good does it do? Airlines are certainly not something managed by dive industry professionals. Shouldn't the size of the industry be evaluated on what dive industry professionals manage?

And here is another problem.

There is a trend away from diving-exclusive vacations. The younger generations are especially more inclined to be doing a bit of scuba diving, among many other activities. Therefore, if one goes to Costa Rica and only does one day of scuba diving, the cost of the airfare and lodging should certainly not be counted as part of the dive industry since only 14% of the week was for scuba diving.

DIVE INDUSTRY EXPENSES VS. GDP

This topic is more of a heads-up.

We regularly see reports floating around with huge numbers about the size of the dive industry. However, when you check the fine print, the authors were actually estimating its total GDP impact.

An evaluation of the full GDP impact includes all direct and indirect spending linked to somebody scuba diving, including what is spent in local restaurants, for instance, and how much the staff of the dive center also spends in the local economy. It's easy to get to a considerable amount!

These over-inflated numbers are often produced by organizations lobbying governmental entities. They need to make the dive industry sound as big as possible to increase their chances of being heard. However, they are misleading figures when trying to assess the size of the dive industry itself.

4: Warning: An Epidemy of Fake Market Data Studies

This is a critical heads-up for your wallet! And a pet peeve of mine. So let's spend a couple of minutes on it.

We regularly get contacted by people interested in finding more information and statistics about the dive industry: private equity analysts, current dive industry executives, dive instructors considering opening a local dive shop, students working on a thesis, private investors, dive shop owners trying to make sense of their financial results in a challenging scuba diving industry, dive gear manufacturers trying to grow their sales, and the list goes on.

They almost invariably ask about a scuba diving industry market study they purchased that doesn't seem to match the reality they see happening in the dive industry.

Here's what I explain to them.

I have news for you: You've been conned!

If you do a quick Google search, you'll find dozens and dozens of these dive industry market studies promising astonishing growth in the years to come. Usually, these dive industry statistics are available for a price varying between $3,000 and $5,000. They sold you the same rosy numbers last year, the year before, and the year before that. And they'll sell you the same ones next year.

I have more news for you: Not everything you read online is true!

In fact, even PADI's website links to one of these bogus market reports! It's mind-boggling how easy it is to spread misinformation nowadays.

You could get more reliable dive industry statistics and market data by giving $40 to your local tarot card reader.

Did you research the credibility of the 'company' to which you were willing to donate five thousand dollars? Let me help you by laying out signs that you were being conned. Then, we'll finally dive into our analysis of the size of the dive industry.

Signs of Fake Scuba Diving Industry Market Statistics

There are plenty of signs that the dive industry market study you are about to purchase is unreliable. You just have to take a step back and consider them.

The Forecast is Always What You Want To Hear

These tempting dive industry market studies always provide a 'positive' outlook for the dive industry. The scuba diving market statistics are always comforting in these reports.

That's what you want to hear, right? You are looking at investing or improving the return on your investment in the dive industry, so you want the market to grow. They wouldn't try to sell you a market study with a decline in the dive industry — you would be less likely to buy it. It's 'Psychology 101' followed by 'How to Manipulate Buyers 102."

Every Industry Forecast on Their Website is Positive

Impressive! Apparently, we live in an era during which every product, in every industry, in every country is booming. Go ahead, invest in anything, and you'll be rich! Yes, this is a sarcastic sentence. More to come!

Seriously, have you checked out the other market studies offered on their website? It's always good news. Every industry is booming, all the time, everywhere in the world. This alone should be a red flag, don't you think?

Their Dive Industry Statistics are Not Just Positive; They Are Over the Top

In press releases that they post all over a bunch of press release websites to boost their SEO, you read explosive sentences like:

"Billion Dollar Global Business with Unlimited Potential"

"Scuba Diving Equipment Market Is Set To Experience Revolutionary Growth By 2030"

Wow! Count me in! I'm selling my house and investing everything I have in that industry. Oh, but, wait… Every industry is like that, based on the market studies available on these websites. I really can invest in everything and anything! It's so cool! I can't wait to count my billions — especially my revolutionary billions!

Seriously, do you know of any industry with 'unlimited' potential? If you do, let me know.

Cloning of Dive Industry Market Studies

Use Big Brother Google. The same report on scuba diving industry statistics is available on numerous websites under different market research company names.

New Scuba Diving Market Studies Every Week

Set up a Google Alert for anything pertaining to scuba diving. You will be notified of press releases every week about a new dive industry market study that looks quite similar to the one announced last week by a different 'company.'

A Fishing Net as a 'Sample'

Go ahead and ask for a 'sample,' then look at it carefully.

4: WARNING: AN EPIDEMY OF FAKE MARKET DATA STUDIES

Basically, you get an extensive table of contents—in other words, you don't get a sample of anything. Furthermore, it looks like they've included everything but the kitchen sink in that table of contents.

It seems as if they took every Google search keyword they could think of and made a chapter out of it. That way, there will be at least one chapter you are interested in. This 'table of contents,' presented as a 'sample,' is a giant fishing net designed to catch as many fish as possible. Can you guess who the fish is?

INSTANT, INFINITE KNOWLEDGE

After receiving such a 'sample,' you will start getting daily email messages offering you the moon. The last time I played the game, these email messages kept asking what else I wanted to see in the report so that I could give them $5000 today.

So, I asked.

I asked about dive regulators in the Republic of Tonga and BCDs in the city of Chicago. Within minutes, I got an email back stating they would add a chapter about that—just like that!

They promised me one chapter would be added to cover what I asked. I wonder how they will mix statistics about scuba regulators in Tonga and BCDs in Chicago. It seems obvious to me that this email reply was an automated reply. It doesn't matter what you ask; they will promise you a chapter about it immediately, just like that, as soon as you send them five thousand dollars.

It must be great to have infinite, instant knowledge about everything, everywhere!

FISHY LINKEDIN PROFILES

Check the LinkedIn profile of the market research company wanting to get $5K from you. If you actually find a company profile, check who the employees are. Does it look credible?

Fortune 500 Clients but No Team

Check the 'About Us' page on their website. There's rarely anybody named there. It's usually generic blah-blah.

They often pretend to have provided market data reports to Fortune 500 companies, yet they have no sales representatives, executives, or teams.

As a general rule of thumb, an 'About Us' page that doesn't tell us anything about who is behind a website is a reason to quickly quit that website — unless you like fishy deals!

If you have nothing to hide, you don't hide.

Dive Industry Segmentation That Makes No Sense

Read the description of these market studies.

You will notice that these people are jam-packing the web page with SEO buzzwords to maximize the chances that Google picks it up when you google for dive industry market statistics. But many of the sentences don't make any sense, grammatically or logically.

You will see statements putting scuba cylinders and masks into the same category of products regularly sold in retail stores. Recompression chambers are also sold in retail stores, apparently – and it's a booming business, of course!

I recently read a summary of a dive industry market study stating that the category of products that they labeled "rebreathers" included snorkels, regulators, and octopuses, while 'apparel' included BCDs.

Come on, people! I know you are eager to find scuba diving industry statistics that could give you hope, but did you answer the Nigerian government official who emailed you to say that he had $10 million to transfer to you?

THE CHERRY ON A SUNDAY OF NONSENSE

Of all the ridiculous announcements I've read about dive industry statistics offered by dubious market research companies, this one I just read today really impresses me because I think a kindergarten kid could have written something less ridiculous.

This is the headline of a press release published in 'Aerospace Journal' (I'm not kidding):

"Snorkeling Equipments Market 2025–2029 | XX% CAGR Projection Over the Next Five Years, Predicts Market Research Future According to Top Investors, Covering Sentimental Industry Analysis, Market Size & Growth"

Well… Eureka! I've been waiting to get a sentimental industry analysis from top investors!

Everything on that website and numerous others is poorly translated into English.

Could you try to explain to me what the following sentence means?

"America accounts for the largest share of the dive tourism market, with the being one of the most significant sources of markets for dive tourism"

Or explain to me this gold nugget:

"Rise in Prevalence of Depression That Boosts The Growth of Scuba Diving Gear Sales Market in Industry"

What? Say that again? I have to admit, I could feel "depressed" when I think of all the money these charlatans are making!

It appears the authors don't bother using spellcheck or grammar check. It seems to me that it's all about using keywords to boost results in Google searches. They probably don't expect anybody to read press releases on that bogus-looking website. Their goal is most likely to boost SEO for the main website where they sell "market studies."

'Aerospace Journal' is a standard WordPress website (they didn't even change the icon) created in 2017 that doesn't seem to contain anything related to aerospace — just a series of 'press releases' about market research covering everything and anything. The press releases link to numerous 'market research companies' all selling the same stuff under different company logos.

Inaccurate Information

Here's another example of nonsense.

I recently read in one of these dive industry market research reports: "In January 2018, the Professional Association of Diving Instructors launched the PADI Travel business aiming to boost growth in the dive industry and to keep divers more engaged and active." Well, PADI Travel has been around for a long time. In January 2018, PADI acquired Diviac, an already existing company, and converted it to 'PADI Travel'.

So, are you willing to pay $5,000 for that kind of highly reliable and earth-shattering knowledge? Yes, this is another sarcastic question.

A Company Living in a Commune

If you manage to find the address of the company trying to get $5,000 from you, do some digging on that address.

Typically, numerous 'market research' companies reside at the same address, all offering very similar market data and forecast reports—and you will rarely find any executive officers for these companies.

A Non-Existing Company

Once you have found a company name and address, perform a search in government records for that company. So far, I have never found any of them in the corporate registry of the country they pretend to be operating out of.

Hopefully, this book will eventually appear higher than the fake reports in search results, and universities will stop sending thousands of dollars to scammers.

But enough of that! Let's start looking at real numbers!

Section 2: Reviewed Market Data & Statistics

5: BEA – Bureau of Economic Analysis

The Bureau of Economic Analysis (BEA) is an agency of the U.S. Department of Commerce. Its mission is to provide accurate and objective data about the U.S. economy, including the famous GDP (Gross Domestic Product).

The BEA provides gross output (G.O.) data measurements by industries. Gross output is a measure of an industry's sales of goods and services.

One industry monitored by the BEA is "outdoor recreation." Within that sector of economic activity, scuba diving is part of "other conventional water activities," which consists of boardsailing, windsurfing, scuba diving, snorkeling, stand-up paddling, surfing, tubing, wakeboarding, water skiing, and whitewater rafting.

For more information: www.bea.gov

Water Activities' Products & Services

First, let's look at the gross output in products and services (excluding travel) for U.S. outdoor recreation in the category "other conventional water activities" in Figure BEA1.

Other conventional water activities' gross output is a bit more than 10 billion dollars per year.

But how do water activities compare to the overall gross output of outdoor recreation?

To answer this question, in Figure BEA2, we look at the BEA total gross output for "conventional outdoor recreation," which excludes activities like amusement parks and festivals. It also excludes economic activities related to travel. In other words, it is a representation of the sales of goods and services (excluding travel) in the outdoor industry in the USA.

The "other water activities" in which scuba diving is included represent less than 3% of the outdoor recreation industry in the USA. Since this water activity category is a catch-all that includes boardsailing, windsurfing, scuba diving, snorkeling, stand-up paddling, surfing, tubing, wakeboarding, water skiing, and whitewater rafting, it is fair to state that scuba diving is a tiny industry.

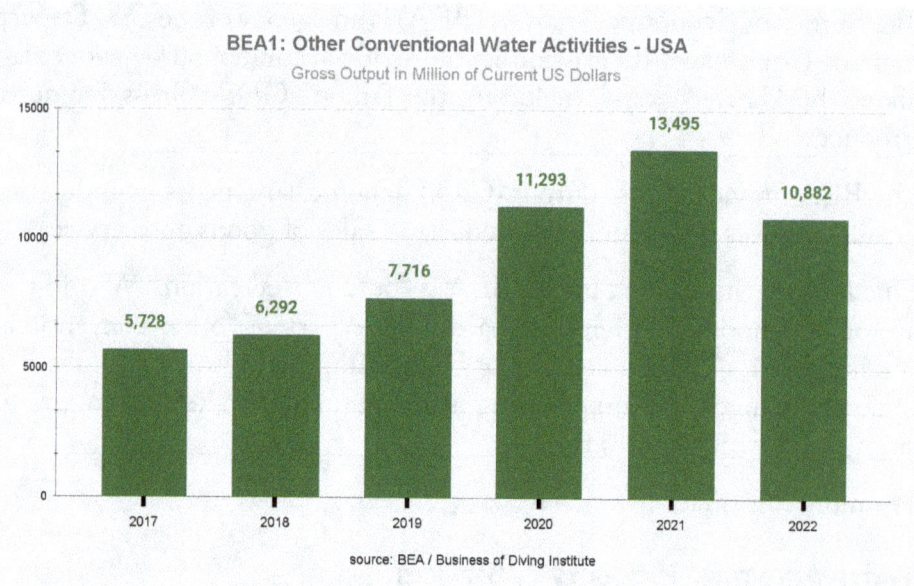

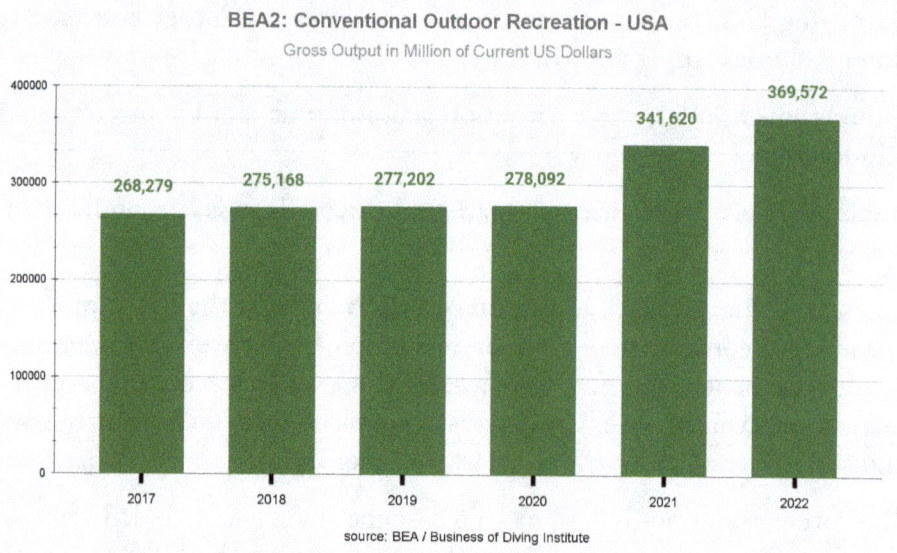

One interesting observation from this data is that the outdoor industry grew during the pandemic while "other outdoor activities" shrank.

To continue putting things in perspective, in Figure BEA3, we compare this "water" category to individual numbers for bicycling, skiing, and snowboarding.

In the last year of available data from the BEA, the size of the catch-all "other water activities" is about equivalent to the sum of bicycling, skiing, and snowboarding. It doesn't tell us anything specific about scuba diving, but it gives us an order of magnitude we can keep in mind when reviewing other sets of data later.

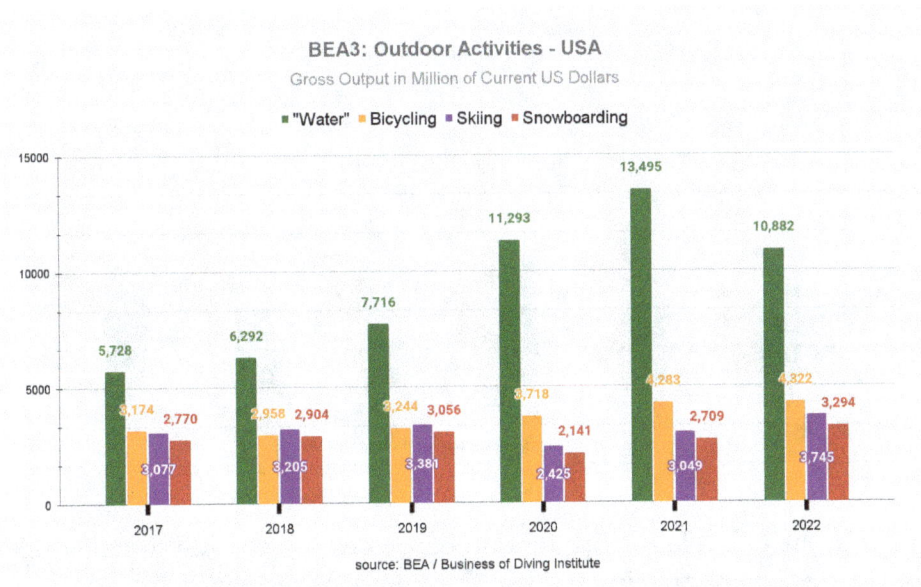

Outdoor Recreation Trips & Travel

Before discussing market data more specific to the dive travel industry, let's examine travel in the overall outdoor recreation industry in the USA with Figure BEA4.

The BEA uses the following definitions:

- **Local trips**: Expenses for trips less than 50 miles (80 km) away from home, including food and beverages, lodging, shopping, souvenirs, and transportation.
- **Travel**: Expenses for tourism with travel at least 50 miles (80 km) away from home.

Since this is market data for gross output in the American economy, these travel expenses do not include travel for outdoor adventures outside the USA, which would be the case for most dive travel.

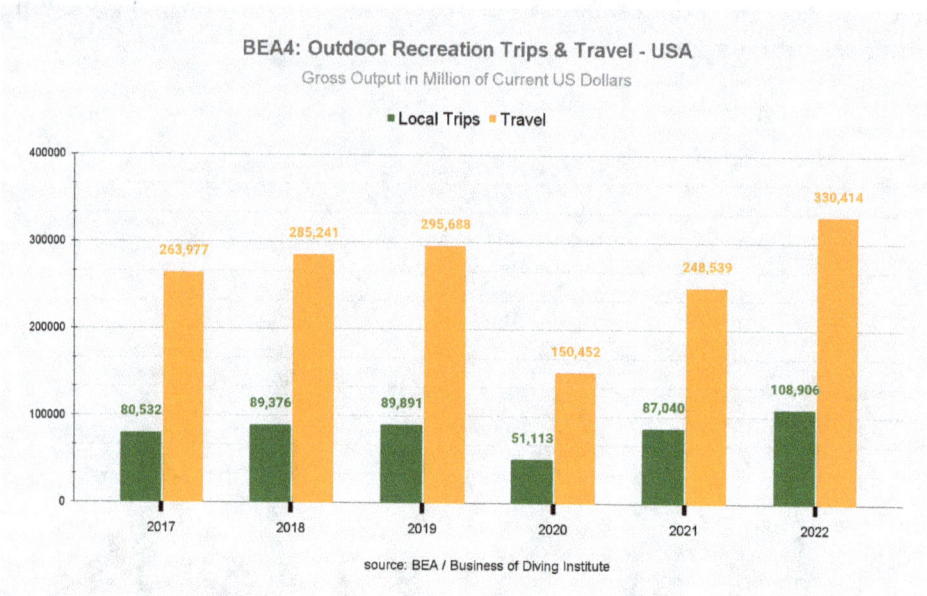

Within the USA, local trips for outdoor recreation account for about 25% of the total spent on trips and travel for outdoor recreation.

Because "local diving" is not very well developed in the dive industry, we could assume that this ratio is lower in our case. Although a fair amount of diving done by residents of Florida, Hawaii, and California falls under the BEA definition of local trips, most scuba diving travel involves international flights to tropical destinations (as opposed to internal flights that would fall within the BEA's travel category). Therefore, the 25% ratio of local trips to total travel may be lower for travel expenses in the dive industry.

Next, in Figure BEA5, let's examine how much of these travel expenses are for lodging and transportation, which is an essential factor to consider when reviewing the dive travel and resort industry.

From the 2022 Bureau of Economic Analysis statistics, here is the percentage of each component within overall travel expenses for outdoor recreation within the USA but more than 50 miles (80 km) from home:

- Food & Beverage: 16%
- Lodging: 22%
- Shopping & Souvenirs: 15%
- Transportation: 48%

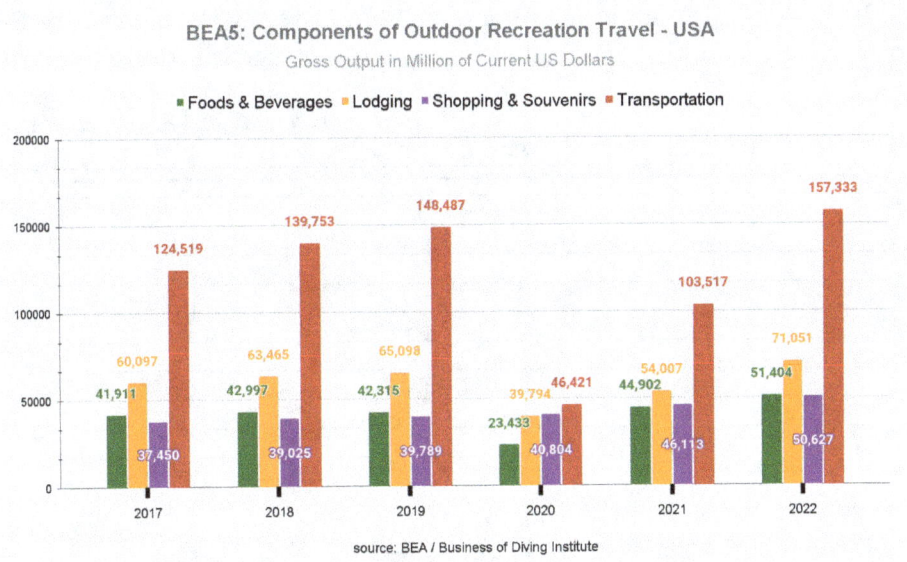

Obviously, transportation is a significant component of any vacation that includes traveling far from home. The numbers in Figure BEA5 are for travel within the USA. Since travel in the dive industry usually involves flying to tropical destinations, we can expect the portion of dive travel allocated to transportation to be higher than 48%.

When evaluating the economic impact of scuba diving on a region's economy, it makes sense to include money spent on food and lodging in non-dive businesses. However, when assessing the size of the dive industry, it doesn't make sense to include these costs and even less to include transportation costs, since these services are provided by companies operating outside the dive industry.

Furthermore, there is a trend toward outdoor enthusiasts doing some scuba diving, among other activities, while on vacation. It makes even less sense to include these travel costs when the whole trip only consists of a day or two of scuba diving.

VALUE-ADDED OUTDOOR RECREATION BY STATE

For those of you interested in the US dive industry, the following table shows each state's outdoor recreation value added as a percent of the state GDP in 2022. The nation's average is 2.2%. Later, we will compare this to each state's ranking in number of scuba diving certifications.

Table BEA6	Outdoor Recreation Value Added as a Percent of the State GDP in 2022
Hawaii:	5.6%
Vermont:	4.6%
Montana:	4.3%
Wyoming:	4.1%
Alaska:	4.0%
Maine:	3.9%
Florida:	3.6%
Indiana:	3.4%
Utah:	3.2%
New Hampshire:	3.2%
Idaho:	3.1%
Colorado:	2.8%
Washington:	2.7%
Nevada:	2.7%
Louisiana:	2.7%
Minnesota:	2.6%

5: BEA – BUREAU OF ECONOMIC ANALYSIS

Table BEA6 — *Outdoor Recreation Value Added as a Percent of the State GDP in 2022*

State	Percent
South Carolina:	2.6%
Oregon:	2.5%
Arizona:	2.5%
South Dakota:	2.5%
Arkansas:	2.5%
Wisconsin:	2.5%
Tennessee:	2.4%
Mississippi:	2.4%
Rhode Island:	2.3%
Missouri:	2.2%
Illinois:	2.1%
Ohio:	2.1%
Georgia:	2.1%
California:	2.0%
Texas:	2.0%
Michigan:	2.0%
Kentucky:	2.0%
Alabama:	2.0%
North Carolina:	2.0%
New Mexico:	1.9%
Kansas:	1.9%
Oklahoma:	1.9%
Iowa:	1.9%
North Dakota:	1.8%
Pennsylvania:	1.8%
Nebraska:	1.7%
Virginia:	1.7%
West Virginia:	1.7%
Maryland:	1.7%

Table BEA6	Outdoor Recreation Value Added as a Percent of the State GDP in 2022
New Jersey:	1.7%
Massachusetts:	1.7%
Delaware:	1.5%
New York:	1.5%
Connecticut:	1.4%
District of Columbia:	0.9%

We will use these BEA figures as a reference point when analyzing the number of scuba diving certifications by state. We expect the dive industry to be more significant in southern coastal states like Florida, Texas, Hawaii, and California. However, these BEA statistics can loosely indicate how "outdoorsy" residents of each state are, and that could also impact scuba diving participation.

6: SFIA: Sport & Fitness Industry Association

SFIA is the Sport & Fitness Industry Association in the USA, formerly the Sporting Goods Manufacturers Association (SGMA).

SFIA conducts annual surveys on multiple sports and fitness activities, including scuba diving, although dive industry stakeholders are not much involved in this association.

SFIA provides us with participation rates for "core" and "casual" scuba divers, which is vital information for dive gear manufacturers and travel operators since core divers typically buy more gear and purchase more dive trips than casual ones.

Here are the definitions used by SFIA:

- **Casual**: went diving 1 to 7 times per year
- **Core**: went diving 8 or more times per year

The SFIA annual participation rates are pretty accurate because they are the results of a random survey of the general population. We will never get a truly precise determination of the size of the dive industry until we do the same, but that is a topic we will address at the end of this book in the "What's Next" section.

In the meantime, if you are interested in scuba diving market statistics and are on a limited budget, cancel your DEMA membership and join the SFIA. You will get much more valuable market information.

If we know how much a diver spends annually on average, then we can multiply that figure by the number of active divers in the market to get one data point on the size of the dive industry. Germany conducted a study along those lines a few years back, and we will look at it later in this book. Otherwise, at the Business of Diving Institute, we tested surveys to accomplish the same in other markets. We will come back to this topic.

We will examine participation rates for scuba diving, obviously, but also for snorkeling and swimming since these are activities with which dive operators and dive gear manufacturers generate revenues. Unfortunately, SFIA does not survey freediving or surface-supplied air diving, and it does not make a distinction for tech diving.

Then, we will examine the participation rate in two other water activities encountered in numerous dive centers: stand-up paddling and surfing.

Finally, we will look at the SFIA report on equipment sales in the USA because it specifically evaluates sales of scuba diving and snorkeling equipment—something we do not even get from our own dive industry trade association, DEMA!

For more information: www.sfia.org

Water Sports Participation

To put water sports in perspective, here are the participation rates by Americans aged 6+ in various categories of activities in 2023.

- Fitness Sports: 68%
- Outdoor Sports: 57%
- Individual Sports: 42%

- Team Sports: 26%
- Racquet Sports: 18%
- Water Sports: 16%
- Winter Sports: 10%

For the SFIA, "outdoor sports" include water sports even though water sports are also reported separately.

Every category experienced growth in participation in 2023.

Scuba Diving Participation

3 million participants represent about 1% of the 6+ American population (0.98%).

In the USA, scuba diving had a good year in 2023, with growth even when compared to pre-pandemic levels. This is something we also observed in our 2024 State of The Dive Industry market report, which we will cover in the next section.

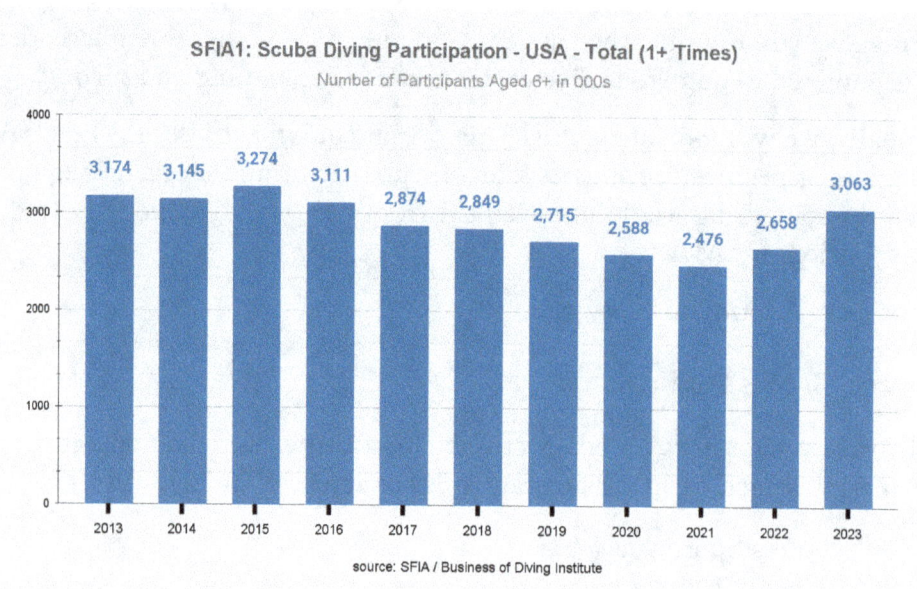

6: SFIA: SPORT & FITNESS INDUSTRY ASSOCIATION

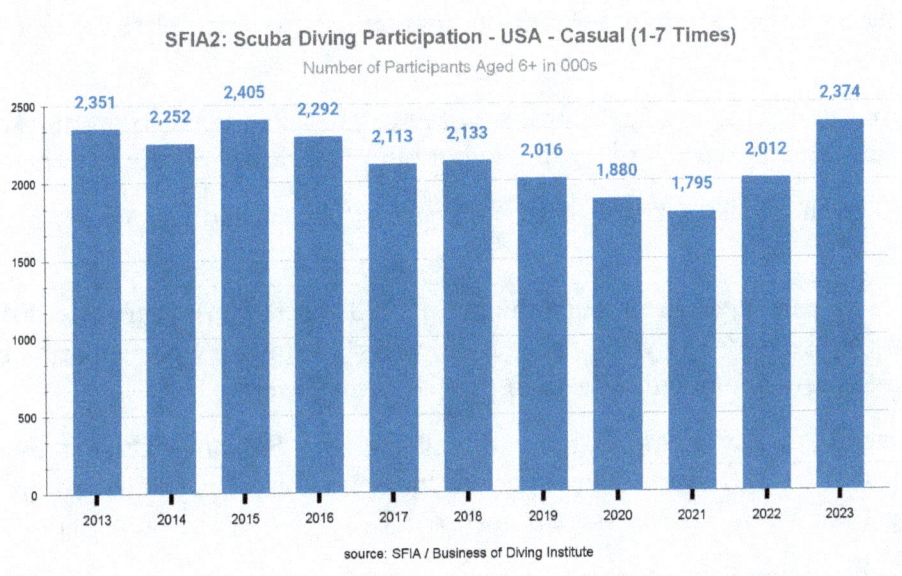

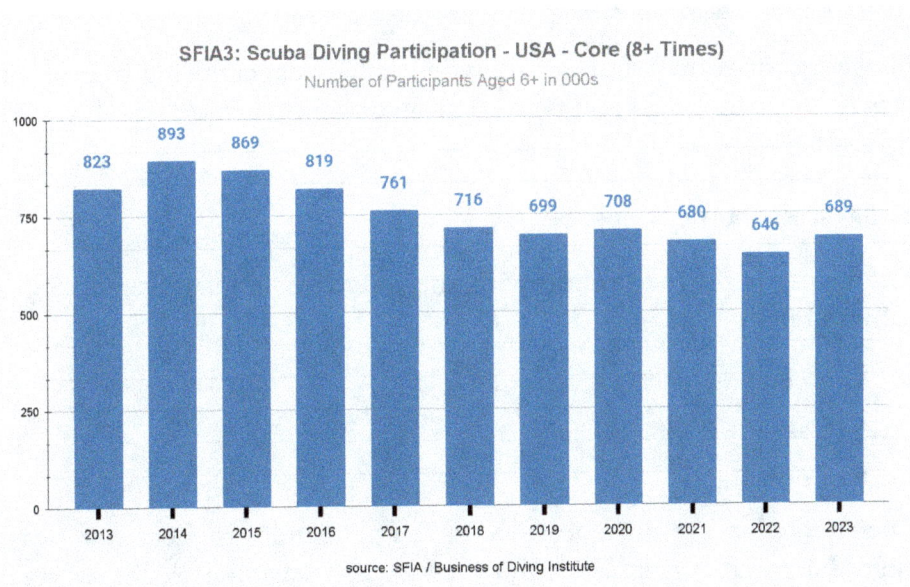

Western Europe also had a good 2023 year but it was not the case in China and Asia-Pacific. Therefore, as we mentioned in the first section of this book, we cannot use American market data to extrapolate to the rest of the world.

However, the more data points we have from various markets around the world, the more we will be able to put our gigantic 3D puzzle together.

An essential factor to note here is that growth in scuba diving comes from casual divers.

Casual participation in scuba diving in 2023 was the best year since 2015 and the second-best year of the last 10 years. Meanwhile, participation by core divers remained lower than pre-pandemic levels.

Overall, scuba diving participation grew by 1.8% on average annual growth (AAG) over a 5-year period. However, casual participation grew by 2.7%, while core participation shrank by 0.7% over the same period.

Scuba diving is not the only activity in which casual participation is on the rise while core participation is on the decline. In sailing, for instance, casual participation was up 4.1% (5-Year AAG) in 2023, while core participation was down 3.2%.

However, there are also water activities that are experiencing tremendous growth in both casual and core participants, like surfing, which we will review below.

Snorkeling Participation

Snorkeling is on the decline with the following annual average 5-year growth rates

- Overall: -0.8%
- Casual: -0.7%
- Core: -1.2%

The snorkeling decline is not due to the pandemic. In fact, there was a slight bump up during 2020. But the big drop started in 2018, two years before the pandemic.

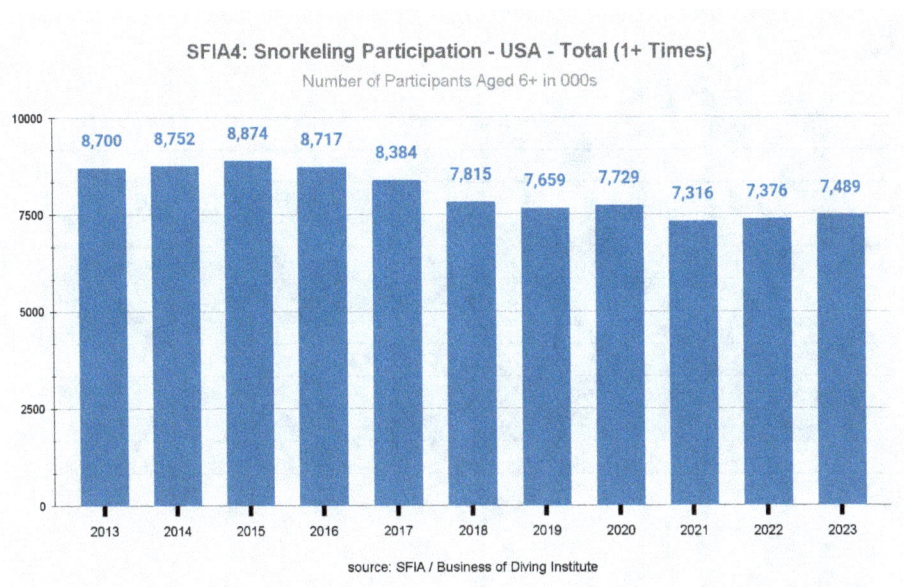

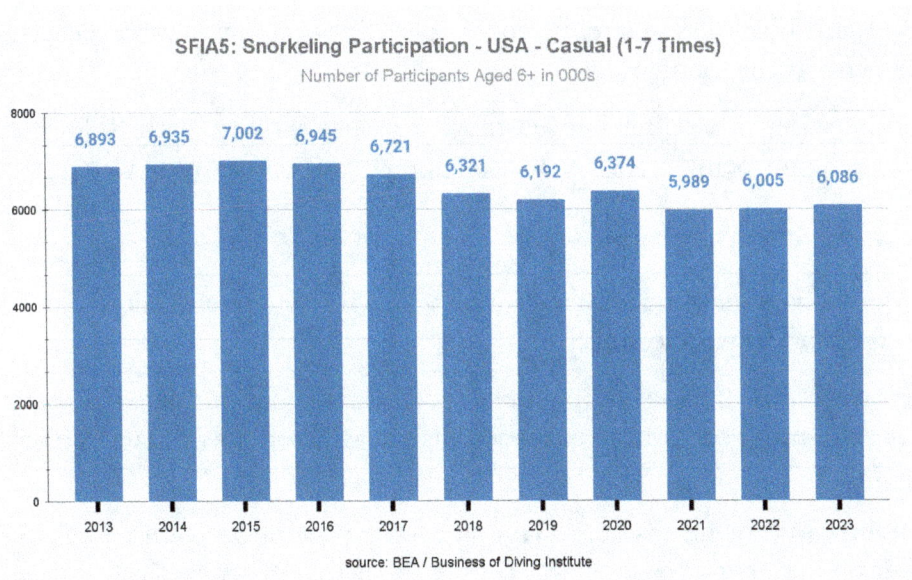

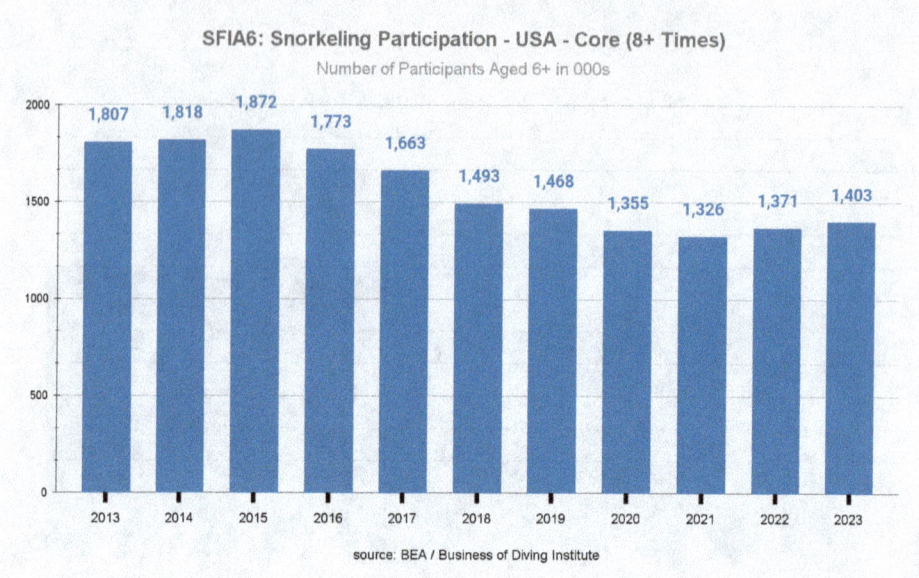

In absolute numbers, there are still more than twice the number of snorkelers than scuba divers. Therefore, dive retailers and manufacturers can still count on snorkeling sales, while dive boat operators can still successfully fill boats for snorkeling tours. But it's not a sector with promising growth at the moment.

Otherwise, snorkeling is even more a casual activity, with 81% of the participants being casual in 2023, while 78% of scuba divers were casual.

Swimming Participation

Many dive shops and manufacturers sell swim equipment, and a few dive centers offer swim lessons.

However, the data we have here is specifically about people participating in swimming for fitness purposes. It can still serve as a data reference point.

Swimming for fitness is growing at a slow pace of 0.6% (5-Year AAG), but the number of participants is nine times that of scuba divers.

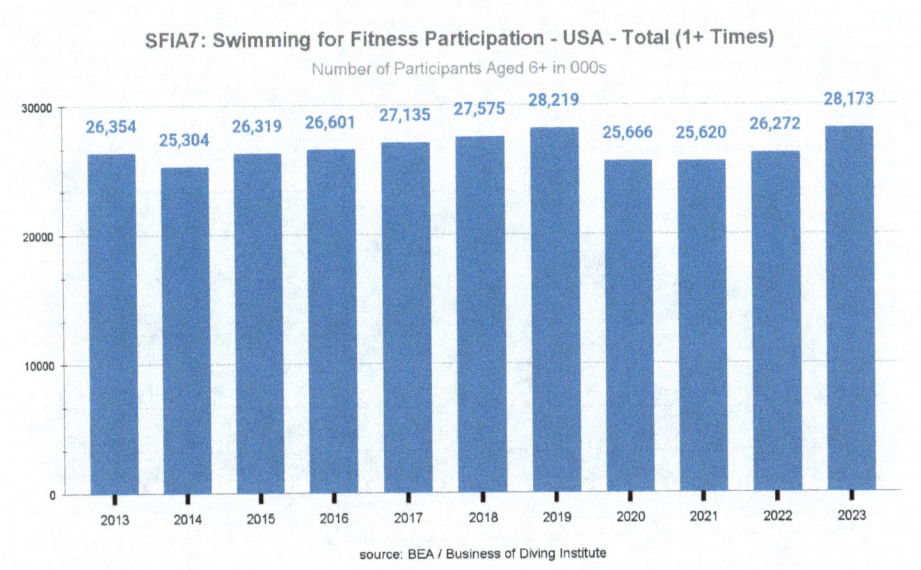

However, what is more promising is that swimming for fitness is an aspirational activity among inactive people of every age group and every income level, while scuba diving and snorkeling are on none.

STAND-UP PADDLING PARTICIPATION

Stand-up paddling (SUP) has steadily grown yearly, and the COVID-19 pandemic didn't stop it.

If you operate a dive shop and you haven't looked at SUP yet, you probably should. And if you operate a dive site, stand-up paddling could be an exciting activity during surface intervals or for spouses who are not scuba diving.

In Lauderdale-by-the-Sea, Florida, we regularly see divers paddling to the reef from shore on a stand-up paddleboard and then towing it with a dive flag on it. My friends at BLU3, a manufacturer of surface-supplied diving equipment, introduced me to this technique, and I love it!

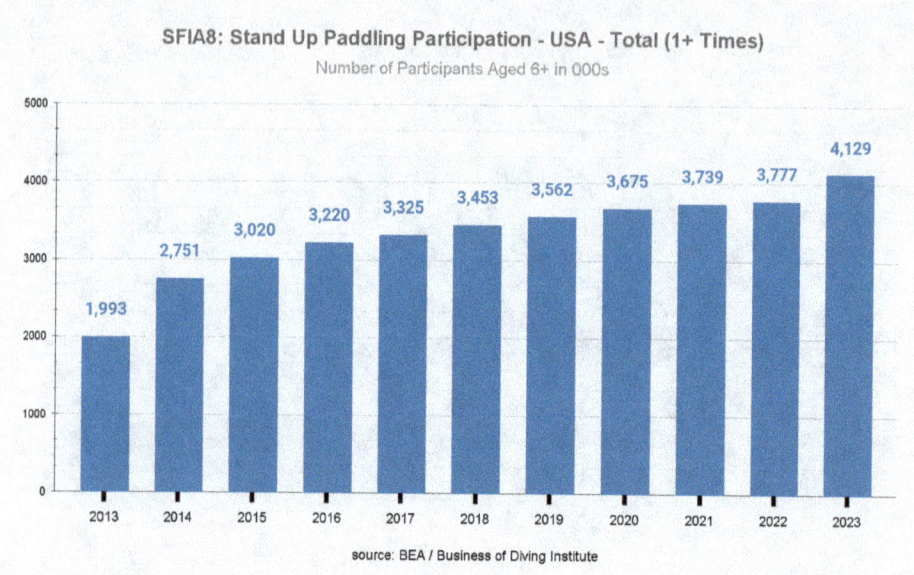

Surfing Participation

Numerous dive centers carry surfing products. In the USA, we especially see such a combo in California and on the mid-Atlantic coast of Florida. Dive'n'Surf is quite famous for it in Redondo Beach, California.

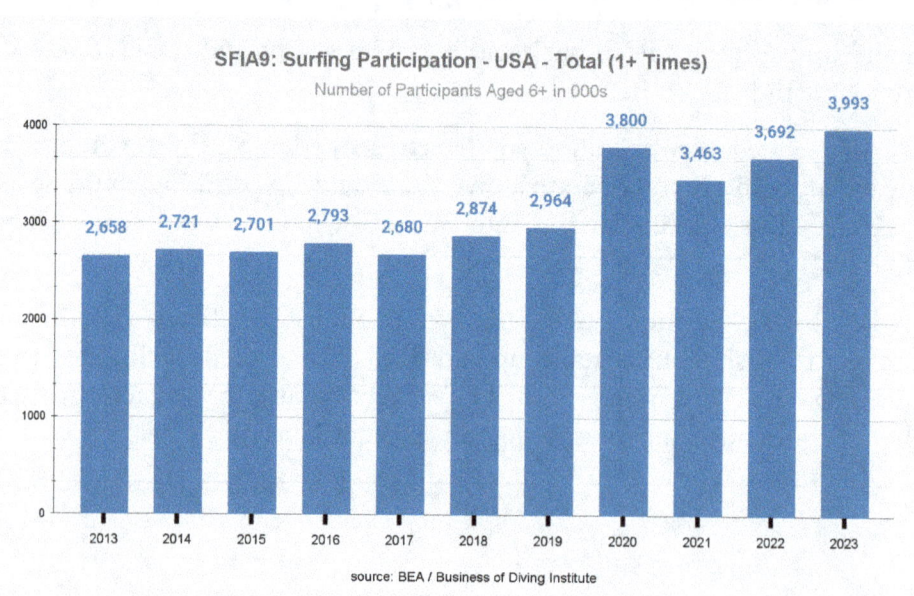

Surfing is a pandemic success story. It simply exploded in 2020! After that, it came back down to earth in 2021 and 2022. Yet, surfing currently shows a 5-year annual average growth rate (AAR) of 7.4%. I know several dive gear manufacturers and dive centers who would love such an increase in sales.

Golf Participation

Before moving on to dive gear sales, as promised, let's take a minute to look at golf.

The dive industry is often compared to golfing because it has traditionally been a white baby boomer activity. So, let's see if golfing is experiencing the same declining or soft growth as scuba diving.

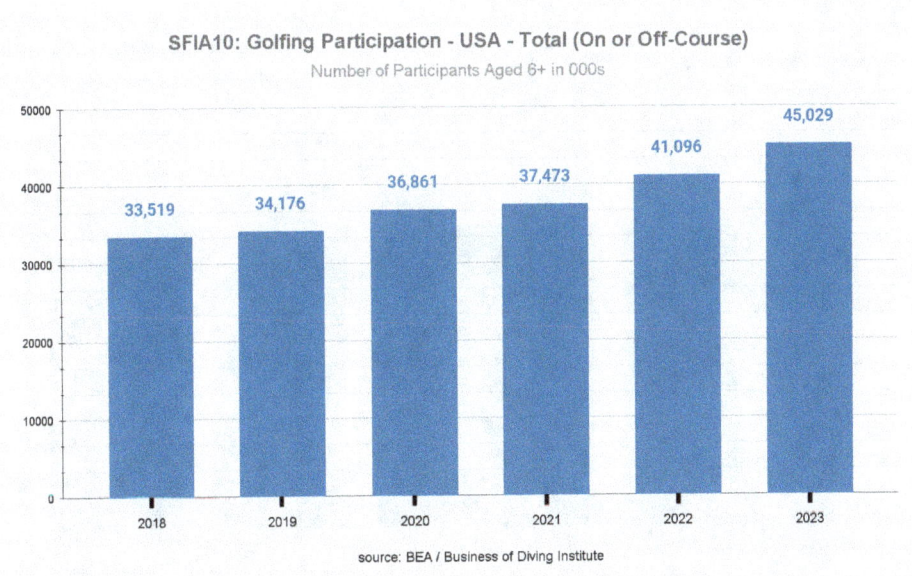

In Figure SFIA10, we see that golf has been growing steadily since 2018, with a 34% jump from 2018 to 2023.

So, yes, it is possible for a traditional "white baby boomer" activity to change and grow. Golfing re-invented itself a few years back, and it is paying off.

The dive industry urgently needs to get back to the drawing board and change both its business model and marketing strategies. However, this goes beyond the scope of this book. Join the conversation at businessofdiving.com.

Dive Gear Manufacturers' Sales

The SFIA survey on gear sales put together scuba and skin diving, also referred to as snorkeling.

The reported dive gear sales in Figure SFIA11 are at the manufacturer (wholesale) level. To estimate what it means at the retail level (to the end-consumer), we can roughly multiply by 2 to 3. Still, it depends on numerous tractors, including the presence or not of a distributor between the manufacturer and the retailer.

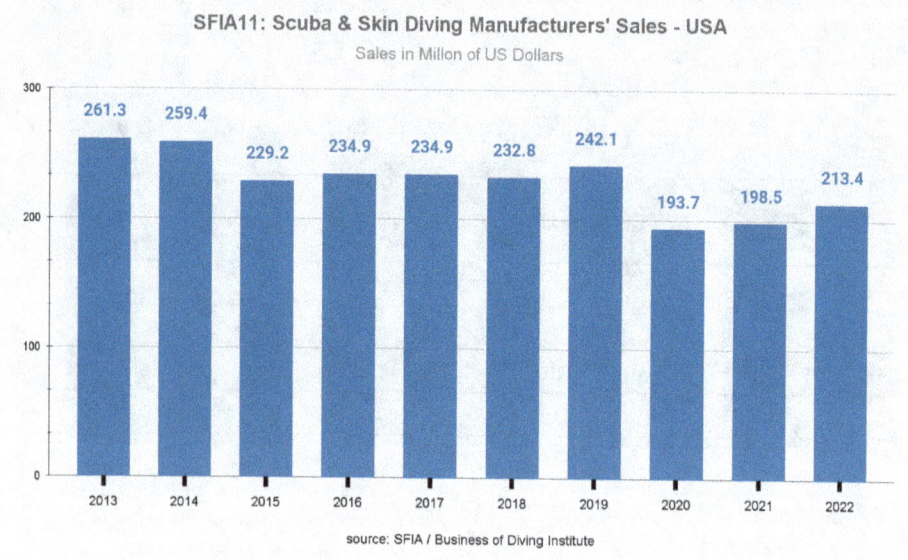

Although dive equipment sales have been growing since the depth of the pandemic in 2020, sales in 2023 remain 11.9% below pre-pandemic levels (2019).

So, there is a disconnect between scuba diving participation that rebounded from the pandemic and dive gear sales that have not. This disconnect may be related to a change in consumer behavior, with casual divers much less inclined to purchase a complete set of dive gear.

Otherwise, the fluctuation in sales by manufacturers may differ from actual retailer sales to end-users because we do not know the fluctuation in inventory on retailers' floors. We will return to these numbers as we review data from other sources.

Socio-demographic Profile of Scuba Divers

We often hear mentions that scuba diving is still predominantly an activity for white male baby boomers. Although we certainly feel that way when attending the DEMA Show, it may no longer be accurate.

Scuba Diving Participation Rate by Age Groups

While overall, 0.98% of the American population went scuba diving at least once last year, people aged between 13 and 44 had a higher participation rate than the baby boomers.

- 13 to 17: 1.1%
- 18 to 24: 1.2%
- 25 to 34: 1.3%
- 35 to 44: 1.2%
- 45 to 54: 0.8%
- 55 to 64: 0.5%
- 65+: 0.2%

Millennials (born from 1981 to 1996) currently have the highest rate of scuba diving participation in the USA.

Scuba Diving Participation Rate by Race

So, scuba diving is no longer a baby boomer activity, but is it still a white male one?

Caucasian Americans actually have a lower scuba diving participation rate than Hispanic and Asian-American.

- Hispanic: 1.0%
- Asian American: 0.9%
- Caucasian: 0.8%
- African American/Black: 0.5%
- Other: 1.2%

SCUBA DIVING PARTICIPATION RATE BY GENDER

Although it is no longer accurate to state that scuba diving is a white baby boomer activity, it is still, unfortunately, mainly a male one.

- Male: 1.0%
- Female: 0.6%

OTHER SCUBA DIVING DEMOGRAPHICS

On the household revenue side, scuba diving has the highest participation rate (1.4%) among households with annual incomes above $100,000.

On the education front, scuba participation is the highest among college graduates (1.1%) and post-graduates (1.2%).

So, in other words, the "stereotype" of a scuba diver in the USA should actually be a Hispanic Millennial male with post-graduate studies and an annual income above $100,000.

7: OIA: OUTDOOR INDUSTRY ASSOCIATION

In the first edition of this book, we extensively reviewed data from the Outdoor Industry Association (OIA) in the USA.

However, OIA and SFIA pool their resources and use the same sub-contractor to do their annual surveys of the American market. Therefore, the OIA survey results are identical to those from the SFIA, and there is no point in repeating them here.

Although we get all the market data from SFIA, you may want to consider membership in OIA since their government lobbying efforts and policy agenda are more closely related to our needs in the dive industry.

Otherwise, the Outdoor Retailer Show is a trade show you may consider attending to view a cross-section of a wide variety of outdoor activities.

For more information: outdoorindustry.org

8: Dive Center Business Magazine

In addition to being a good source of management advice for dive center owners, Dive Center Business (DCB) magazine is the most reliable source of information on the number of dive centers in the USA.

For more information: divecenterbusiness.com

Number of Dive Centers in the USA

There is no official count on the number of dive centers in the USA, and even less globally.

And the problem starts with the definition of a dive center! Many "dive centers" listed on dive training agencies' "store locators" are nothing more than a few square feet of space in a dive instructor's personal garage at home.

Meanwhile, the team at DCB keeps a rigorous list of dive centers in the USA where they mail, for free, the Dive Center Business magazine. If a dive store goes out of business, the mail usually bounces back.

DCB defines a dive center as a business with a retail storefront, compressor on site, full-line equipment sales, and training.

These are the DCB numbers over the years:

- 2000: 1924 dive center businesses in the USA
- 2013: that number was down to 1530
- 2019: approximately 1425 (about 75% of the 2000 level)

The number of dive centers in the USA has been systematically going down year after year.

For instance, in 2019, the last full pre-coronavirus year, 58 dive stores closed in the USA while 43 new ones opened, for a net decrease of 15

American dive centers. Over the period of 1999 to 2019, 1,486 new stores opened while 1,909 closed, for a net loss of 423 dive centers.

The dive industry can no longer depend on local dive shops to grow, but this is a business model discussion that goes beyond the scope of this market study.

Impact of The COVID-19 Pandemic

The Business of Diving Institute estimates that about 25% of American dive centers permanently closed during the pandemic.

Although the SFIA scuba diving participation rate indicates that scuba diving is back to pre-pandemic levels in the USA, we do not expect the number of "real" dive centers to go back to pre-pandemic levels as scuba divers' shopping habits are changing.

With the steady annual decline that started before the pandemic, in addition to the economic shock of COVID-19, we estimate that the number of dive centers in the USA is around 1000.

9: Leisure Trends

Leisure Trends used to produce reports on gear sales in the dive industry by collecting data directly at the cash register of a sample of dive retail businesses in the USA. Therefore, the market data was pretty accurate. However, it was skewed upwards because, at the time, only the best dive centers had a point-of-sale system sophisticated enough to be connected to this survey.

It is an issue we notice in pretty much every dive industry survey. They usually tend to be skewed toward the positive side because it is the best dive operators who participate in these surveys.

Leisure Trends stopped doing this market survey in the mid-2000s, presumably because there were not enough dive industry paying subscribers for the reports they produced. It was expensive. Since then, Leisure Trends has been purchased by NPD Group which later merged with IRI and rebranded as Circana.

9: LEISURE TRENDS

We have been able to forensically reconstitute some of the data from the mid-2000s, which can give us some indication of the size of the dive industry at that point in time and, more specifically, the split of sales between various product categories.

Obviously, the size of dive centers has changed since then, and so has their mix of products and services.

Later in this book, we will share current figures from recent market surveys conducted by the Business of Diving Institute. By comparing our recent survey results to these old Leisure Trends figures, we will see the evolution of the dive industry over the last twenty years.

For more information: www.circana.com

Dive Gear Retail Sales

Leisure Trends evaluated that in 2006, dive equipment retail sales by dive shops totaled 438 million dollars.

This would mean wholesale sales of about $220 million from manufacturers, brands, and distributors. However, these are only sales through local dive shops. They do not include dive gear sales through other channels. Therefore, the actual size of the dive gear market in the USA in 2006 was superior to this $438 million figure.

In comparison, SFIA has the total size of the wholesale dive gear market pegged at $213 million for 2022, but this figure also misses some parts of the market, especially imports.

We will come back to this.

Total Dive Retail Sales

Leisure Trends statistics indicated that the size of total retail sales done by dive centers in the USA was about 875 million dollars annually. This number included:

- Gear
- Training

- Trips & Travel
- Other Services

Unfortunately, under trips and travel, some fly-away travel sales were included. Most dive centers do not record these travel sales in their store revenues because they are not licensed travel agents, but the fact that some dive shops did end up skewing sales results.

As we have seen in statistics from BEA, transportation and lodging are the most significant expenses in travel to destinations far from home. It is best not to include these numbers when evaluating the size of the dive industry, as these revenues are, for the most part, received by entities outside the dive industry.

Here is what we have been able to reconstruct by eliminating fly-away travel.

Average Revenues per Dive Center

In 2006, the average American dive store had revenues of $355 thousand for all products & services.

We will share an update from the most recent State of the Dive Industry survey later in this book.

Split of Revenues by Categories in Local Dive Shops

Here is the average sales split between each category of products and services sold in a local dive shop in 2006.

Table LT1 *Split of Revenues by Category*

Equipment:	54.8%
Training:	20.0%
Local Dive Outings:	8.7%
Repair & Maintenance:	7.9%
Renting Gear:	5.7%
Other:	2.9%

This was a national average. Even today, some dive shops may have results significantly different from the national average. For instance, a dive center in Key Largo, Florida, would have a much more significant percentage of its revenues coming from local dive outings (dive charters) than a dive center in landlocked Las Vegas.

Later, we will see that over the years, the percentage of revenues from sales of dive gear has been steadily shrinking.

SPLIT OF DIVE GEAR REVENUES BY TYPE

Table LT2	*Split of Revenues from Equipment Sales*
Scuba Units:	27.7%
Fins, Masks & Snorkels:	18.6%
Exposure Suits:	15.2%
Non-Essentials:	36.1%
Cylinders:	2.5%

The table above gives us the split of dive gear sales among different types of equipment in an average dive shop in the USA in 2006. In the table below, we further split revenues among parts of the scuba unit.

Table LT3	*Split of Revenues from Sales of Scuba Units (totalling 27.7% of gear sales)*
BCDs:	7.8%
Regulators:	9.1%
Computers & Gauges:	10.6%
Rebreathers:	0.2%

And the following table gives us more detail on the sales of what was considered non-essentials in 2006.

Table LT4	Split of Revenues by Sales of Non-Essentials (36.1% of gear sales)
Photo & Video Equipment:	3.4%
Dive Propulsion Vehicles:	0.2%
Bags & Luggage:	3.8%
Apparel:	3.4%
Dive Accessories:	25.3%

DIVE TRAINING STATISTICS

In 2006, the average price of a course (any course) was $308 in the USA.

421 thousand certifications were issued in 2005 at all levels. These certifications were split as follows:

- 64% entry-level
- 32% continuing education
- 4% leadership

For your general information, the following table presents an overview of the popularity of dive training agencies in 2006.

Table LT5	Percentage of Dive Centers Affiliated With Each Training Agency
PADI:	58.6%
NAUI:	19.2%
SSI:	18.4%
YMCA:	4.9%
NASDS:	4.1%
TDI:	3.8%
IANTD:	3.8%
PDIC:	2.2%
NASE:	1.1%
ANDI:	0.8%

Table LT5 *Percentage of Dive Centers Affiliated With Each Training Agency*

NSSCDS:	0.8%
MDEA:	0.5%
Other:	0.8%

These percentages represent the number of dive centers issuing some certifications with those training agencies. Since a dive center may use more than one training agency, the total is more than 100%.

10: U.S. Census Bureau

The U.S. Census Bureau compiles numerous statistics, including data on imports and exports, by category of products.

Unfortunately, in the USA, there is only one category of imported products defining a specific scuba gear category: regulators.

Every other scuba product is imported in a category that includes numerous other non-diving products. For instance, buoyancy compensators (BCD) are imported under code 9506.29.0040, which is used for: "Water skis, surfboards, sailboards, and other water sports equipment."

For more information: www.census.gov

Dive Regulator Imports

Scuba diving regulators are well defined for imports under category 9020.00.4000: "Underwater breathing devices designed as a complete unit to be carried on the person and not requiring attendants."

In Figure USC1, we see the dollar value of regulators imported by wholesalers in the USA. With both the wholesaler and retailer taking a markup, we can estimate the retail value of these regulators to be about three times the import value.

This would translate into retail sales of $31.5M in 2023.

But for numerous reasons, we cannot rely on that figure.

First, not all imported regulators are sold at retail during the same year, and we do not know the inventory fluctuations of dive gear at wholesalers and retailers.

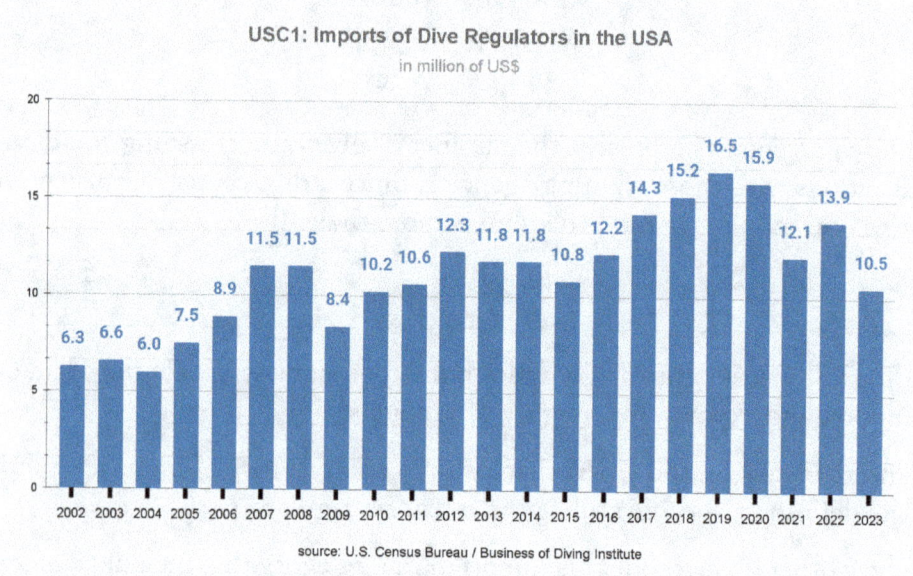

Otherwise, the U.S. Census Bureau statistics include regulators imported for commercial and military diving.

Finally, some regulators are manufactured in the USA.

Dive Regulator Exports

In the following figure, we see the value of regulators exported from the USA.

In Figure USC2, we notice considerable fluctuations in the value of regulators exported from the USA. These export values include regulators that were imported and then re-exported, as well as regulators manufactured in the USA for export.

Just like in the case of imports, the U.S. Census Bureau statistics include regulators sold for commercial and military diving. A single military order can represent a significant amount.

And there are many other possible reasons for these considerable swings in the value of regulator exports, like OEM production.

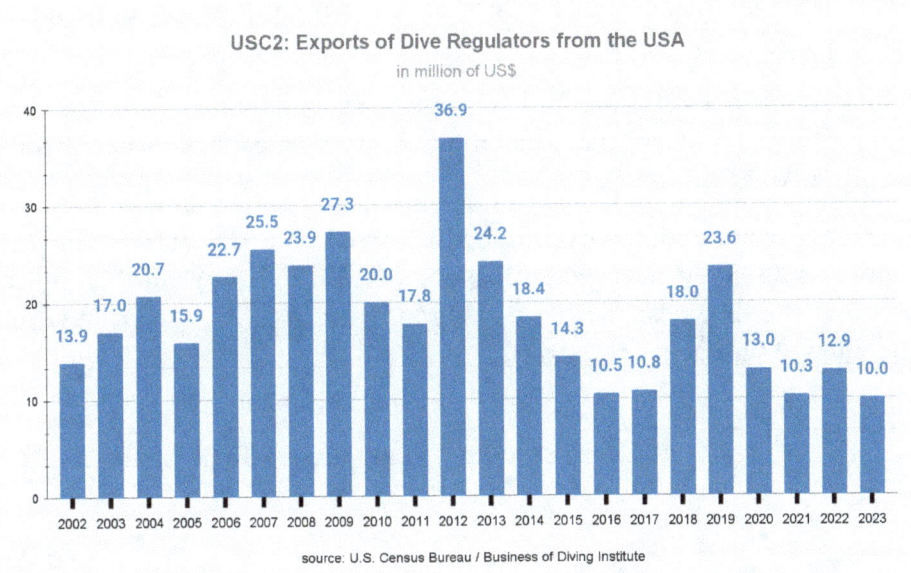

Either way, in short, there is, unfortunately, not much we can learn from the value of regulator import and export.

11: Dive Gear Manufacturers & Brands

Market data for the dive industry is scarce, which applies to dive gear manufacturers and brands. Only two dive equipment brands, Scubapro (Johnson Outdoors) and Brownie's Marine Group have official financial reports available because they are publicly traded.

Mares' parent company used to be publicly traded but is not anymore.

Some of Beuchat's numbers are available because of financial reporting requirements in France. And some Aqua Lung numbers were leaked in the process of Air Liquide selling its diving division to Montagu.

Scubapro (Johnson Outdoors)

Scubapro is the only major dive gear brand for which we have regular and reliable financial numbers because it is part of Johnson Outdoors, a publicly traded company.

Scubapro revenues (Figure MAN1) represent worldwide sales to retailers or distributors. We estimate that about 75% of Scubapro's revenues come from the American market.

Sales have fluctuated, but overall, Scubapro rebounded well from the pandemic. Its 2023 revenues were the best since 2012. This is another indication that the dive gear market had a good year in 2023, except in China and a few Asia-Pacific countries.

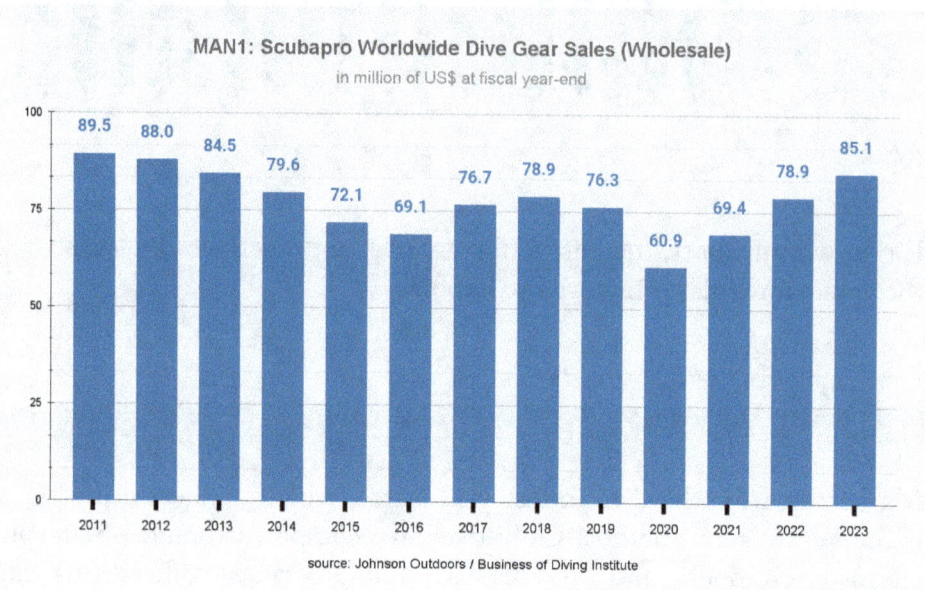

MAN1: Scubapro Worldwide Dive Gear Sales (Wholesale)
in million of US$ at fiscal year-end
source: Johnson Outdoors / Business of Diving Institute

Mares & SSI

Mares is a dive equipment manufacturer owned by the Head Group.

Up to the fiscal year 2008, Head filed annual reports with the SEC but stopped its U.S. listing in 2009. It continued to be publicly traded on the Vienna Stock Exchange until its delisting in March 2015 after its shareholders voted against increasing its capital to meet the exchange's minimum listing requirements. Since then, we no longer have access to detailed annual financial reports.

Even if we did, Head's diving revenues are no longer strictly from diving gear as they have made other acquisitions, including:

- 100% of SSI in January 2014 for Euros 4.9M. It's a dive training agency.
- 100% of rEvo (closed circuit rebreather) in July 2016 for €1.1M plus a 2nd payment in 2019 estimated at €1.6M.
- 67.93% of Liveaboard.com in 2019 for €6.1M.

Mares revenues from the last years of SEC filings are presented in Figure MAN2. It includes revenues for Mares and Dacor, a brand that no longer exists.

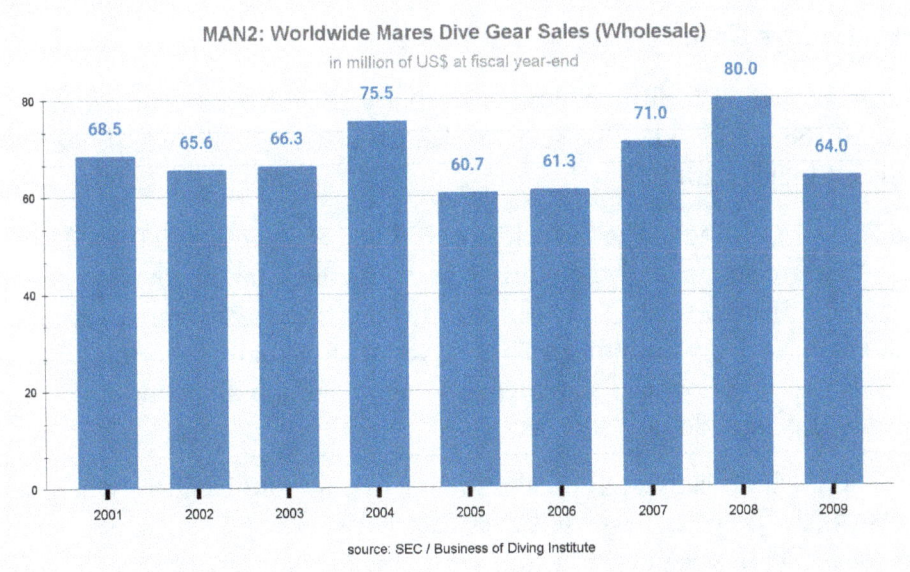

Mares revenues for the last four years of available financial data are in Figure MAN3. Keep in mind that SSI revenues were added to Head's scuba diving sales starting in 2014. And rEvo sales were added in 2016.

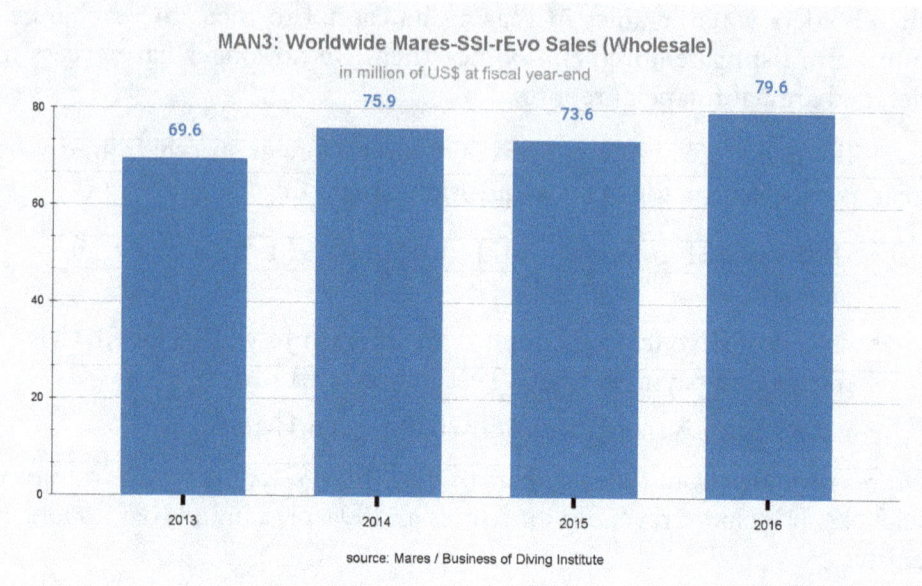

World Dive Gear Market as per Mares

In its annual SEC filings, Mares regularly provided an estimate on the size of the worldwide dive gear market. The last year for which we have this estimate is 2008.

In 2003, in a filing to the Security & Exchange Commission (SEC) in the USA, Mares estimated the worldwide wholesale market for dive gear at US$470 million. In the same filing, Mares estimated having a 17% market share, which would mean $80M. Yet, they actually reported $66.3M in sales in their financial statements. Welcome to the dive industry, where numbers never add up!

In 2008, Mares estimated the worldwide market for dive gear (wholesale) at $676M. They also assessed their market share at 14%, which would mean $95M in revenues. But in their financial results, they reported sales of $77M.

When looking at these numbers over numerous years, it appears that Mares was pretty systematically claiming that the worldwide dive gear market was about 25% bigger than their market share and financial reports indicated.

BEUCHAT

Beuchat is a French dive gear manufacturer. It is not publicly traded, but some French financial reporting requirements allow us to access its annual sales.

In 2022, Beuchat's revenues were €12.8M, approximately $14M.

Just like Mares, their revenues are not "pure diving." They have product lines for swimming in addition to scuba diving, freediving, and spearfishing. More recently, in 2021, Beuchat acquired the triathlon brand Aquaman. It will be even more difficult in years to come to identify Beuchat's dive sales.

AQUA LUNG

For a while, before Montagu destroyed the company, Aqualung was assumed to be the largest dive gear manufacturer and wholesaler in the world.

Up until 2016, Aqua Lung was owned by Air Liquide, a publicly traded company. However, in Air Liquide's financial annual reports, Aqua Lung was buried in the same division as welding products, making it impossible to know how Aqua Lung was performing.

In the process of selling Aqualung to private equity firm Montagu, previously known as HSBC Private Equity, some financial information was either shared or leaked. In 2016, Sporting Goods Intelligence magazine estimated Aqua Lung's revenues at €103M ($113M). Furthermore, it was estimated that about 40% of these revenues were from the USA.

Earlier, an estimate from 2003 had Aqua Lung's annual revenues at $200 million.

Like Beuchat, Aqualung has an extensive line of non-diving products, so these figures are not "purely" for diving.

Brownie's Marine Group

Brownie's Marine Group is a smaller dive gear manufacturer, but it is a publicly traded company, so we have access to their financial numbers. It specializes in surface-supplied air diving systems.

For fiscal year 2022, it declared $8.6M in revenues, an increase of more than 37% over the prior year.

Decathlon

Decathlon is a French sporting goods retailer that sells scuba diving and snorkeling equipment. Its significance for us is that the majority of its products are in-house brands. It designs, manufactures, and sells its own line of products under the brand name Subea.

Since the entire process is in-house, these numbers are generally not accounted for by official surveys on the size of the dive industry. And Decathlon is not a negligible entity, with annual retail sales of €15.4 billion in 2022 (16.9 billion US dollars), which is about the entire size of the worldwide dive industry, including gear, training, and travel!

Decathlon's impact is growing around the world. They have retail operations in 59 countries. In 2017, they announced their first Canadian locations. On the American side, they opened stores in California in 2020 to close them all in 2022. However, Decathlon remains active in the USA with online sales and partnerships with other retailers.

We can expect Decathlon to gradually become a significant player in the snorkeling and diving industry in North America, just like it is already in Europe.

Dive Gear Manufacturers Wrap-Up

Among other reference points, up to a couple of years ago, we estimated sales of Suunto dive computers at about $10M in the USA. However, it is in a bit of turmoil after changing hands a couple of times and being acquired in 2022 by Liesheng, a Chinese group.

We estimate worldwide annual sales of Shearwater dive computers at about $25M. In early 2021, BRS & Co. acquired a controlling interest in Shearwater. BRS & Co is a New York-based private equity firm.

For the handful of companies for which we have financial information, we get close to $400M in annual worldwide wholesale revenues. And we haven't looked at numerous other major dive gear brands like Tusa and all the Huish Outdoor brands (Zeagle, Bare, Oceanic, Atomic, Hollis, and Stahlsac).

Therefore, the worldwide wholesale dive gear market is obviously worth more than $400M per year.

The biggest interrogation mark in terms of the size of the dive gear market is China, where many Chinese manufacturers supply the needs of Chinese scuba divers.

Later in this report, we will combine all the numbers to reach a conclusion.

12: RSTC Europe

RSTC Europe is the Recreational Scuba Training Council for Europe.

In a 2006 report, RSTC Europe stated the following:

- 15M active divers around the world, with 3 to 4M from Europe.

Since we had about 3M active divers in the USA at that time and 3.6M in Europe, this would mean 8.4M active divers (56% of the total) in "the rest of the world." It is doubtful. It is more likely that 15M is extremely overstated or that the RSTC had a very lax definition of "active."

- European dive gear market: €190 million at retail for Europe.

As we will see in the TIV chapter, we have €85 million in dive gear sales in Germany. It would mean that Germany is 45% of Europe, which is ludicrous. It appears RSTC Europe's numbers are unreliable.

- 225K entry-level certifications in Europe per year.

From TIV (in the next chapter), we have Germany at 44K, which would be 19.6% of the market, while its population is 11.1%. We believe scuba diving is more popular in Germany than in other European countries, so it is possible.

- 187K advanced-level training
- 58.7K dive instructors

This would mean that 48% of all European certifications are entry-level ones.

But overall, it seams that the RSTC numbers should simply not be used because they do not appear reliable.

For more information (or lack thereof): www.rstc-eu.org

13: TIV Tauchsport Industrieverband – Germany

Dive industry market data is even more complex to get in Europe than it is in the USA.

However, for Germany, we have market data from Tauchsport Industrieverband (TIV), which means "Dive Industry Association."

From the TIV, we get information on the size of the scuba diving market in Germany in a "Diving in the Future" report published in 2010 and updated in 2015 with market data from 2014, as well as from dive gear sales figures for the year 2015.

For more information: www.tauchsportindustrieverband.de

Dive Gear Sales – Germany

TIV estimates diving equipment sales in Germany to total €85 million per year at retail and €31.8 million at wholesale. This means a retail margin of about 60%. It makes sense as 50% is usually the minimum a retailer will take, but soft goods like accessories, fins, masks, and snorkels usually produce more substantial margins.

Dive Gear Sales – Europe

Suppose we extrapolate Germany's dive gear sales to Europe based on Germany's population being 11% of Europe. In that case, we get dive gear sales in Europe of €289 million at wholesale, which is approximately $317M at the time of writing this analysis.

But this would be overstated because scuba diving is more popular in Germany than in many other European countries.

France, Germany, the UK, and Italy are four countries where scuba diving is more popular than the European average.

It would be more reliable to estimate Germany as 15% of the European market, which would peg the European dive gear market at €162 million at wholesale.

However, as we have mentioned a few times already, such an industry-generated figure does not include the full extent of the scuba, snorkeling, and freediving markets.

Split of Dive Gear Revenues by Type

Table TIV1	USA Leisure Trends 2006	Germany TIV 2015
Scuba Units:	27.7%	38.9%
Fins, Masks & Snorkels:	18.6%	10.8%
Exposure Suits:	15.2%	16.6%
Non-Essentials:	36.1%	27.6%
Cylinders:	2.5%	6.0%

In Table TIV1, we see the split of dive gear sales by type of gear compared to figures we have already reviewed from Leisure Trends. It would appear Germans spend more than Americans on their scuba unit (regulators, BCDs, and instruments), while Americans spend more than Germans on fins, masks, snorkels, and accessories.

Table TIV2 further splits gear sales by product types within the scuba unit category. Germans appear to spend more on regulators and instruments (computers & gauges) than Americans.

Table TIV2	USA Leisure Trends 2006	Germany TIV 2015
BCDs:	7.7%	8.3%
Regulators:	9.1%	13.8%
Computers & Gauges:	10.6%	16.9%
Rebreathers:	0.2%	n/a

However, these two studies were almost 10 years apart. We will come back to this topics later in this book.

Entry-Level Certifications

TIV estimates that 40K people received entry-level certifications in Germany in 2014. This does not include German residents getting a scuba diving certification outside Germany and never interacting with a German dive industry entity.

Participation

TIV segments active scuba divers along the following lines:

- **Leisure Divers**: They do not own a complete set of dive equipment (only partly equipped).
- **Scuba Divers**: They own a complete set of diving equipment (either for warm or cold water).

For comparison purposes, we could roughly estimate that TIV's German "scuba divers" are similar to "core divers" from the SFIA American reports.

Furthermore, TIV defines a category of:

- **Infrequent Divers**: They do not own scuba diving equipment and do not spend at local diving shops in Germany, but use what scuba diving offers on holiday.

Some former "scuba divers" and "leisure divers" fall eventually into the "leisure divers" category.

We see participation by Leisure and Scuba Divers in Table TIV3.

Table TIV3	2009	2014	
Leisure Divers:	230K	229K	-0.4%
Scuba Divers ("core"):	190K	177K	-6.8%
Total:	420K	406K	-3.3%

Just like in the USA (see SFIA), the group of core divers is shrinking faster than casual divers. This has significant consequences for the dive industry, as core divers purchase more dive gear and travel than casual divers.

With Germany's population at 84M, this means a participation rate of 0.5% compared to 0.8% of Americans (SFIA). The relatively lower participation rate in Europe is part of the reason why the dive industry in Europe is smaller per capita than in the USA.

Otherwise, TIV estimates that more than 1.2 million Germans have passed an initial diving instruction, and therefore, the "infrequent divers" would be about 300K people.

Of course, on top of that, there are all the people who have simply tried scuba diving (resort diving or discover scuba diving) and never got a diving certification. This number is enormous, and we will address it later in this book.

Gear Expenses by Diver & New Diver in Germany

The TIV estimates of dive gear spending by German divers are presented in Table TIV4.

	Table TIV4	Initial	Annual
Leisure Divers:		€230	€100
Scuba Divers ("core"):		€2,500	€250

In Germany, a core diver spends more than ten times that of a casual diver on an initial set of dive gear. We see a similar ratio in other markets, and since new divers are more likely than ever to be casual divers, scuba training revenues grow at a faster rate than dive gear sales.

These figures from the TIV mean that about 40% of dive gear sales in Germany are to new divers getting certified.

TRAINING EXPENSES PER DIVER IN GERMANY

	Table TIV5	Initial	Annual
Leisure Divers:		€400	€90
Scuba Divers ("core"):		€400	€170

TIV estimated that the total market size of dive training in Germany was €42.65 million per year.

Extrapolated to Europe based on population size, it would mean that the dive training European market is about €383M. A more realistic estimate pegging the German market at 15% of the European market would mean €218 million.

TRAVEL EXPENSES PER DIVER IN GERMANY

	Table TIV6	Annual
Leisure Divers:		€200
Scuba Divers ("core"):		€1,400

In Table TIV6, we see that the TIV estimated the total market size of dive travel in Germany is €312 million per year.

Extrapolated to Europe based on population size, it would mean that the dive travel European market is about €2.8 billion. A more conservative estimate pegging the German market at 15% of the European market would represent €2 billion.

14: DEMA Diving Equipment & Marketing Association

The Diving Equipment & Marketing Association (DEMA) is the American dive industry trade association. It is a relatively good source of data on entry-level scuba diving certifications in the USA.

For more information: www.dema.org

Dive Gear Sales

DEMA used to produce the Dive Equipment Manufacturing Sales Index (MSI), but it stopped around 2015. Since then, DEMA has provided no information whatsoever on dive gear sales except for a survey on trends but not on the actual volume of sales.

There are two things to learn from the last set of MSI data presented in Figure DEMA1.

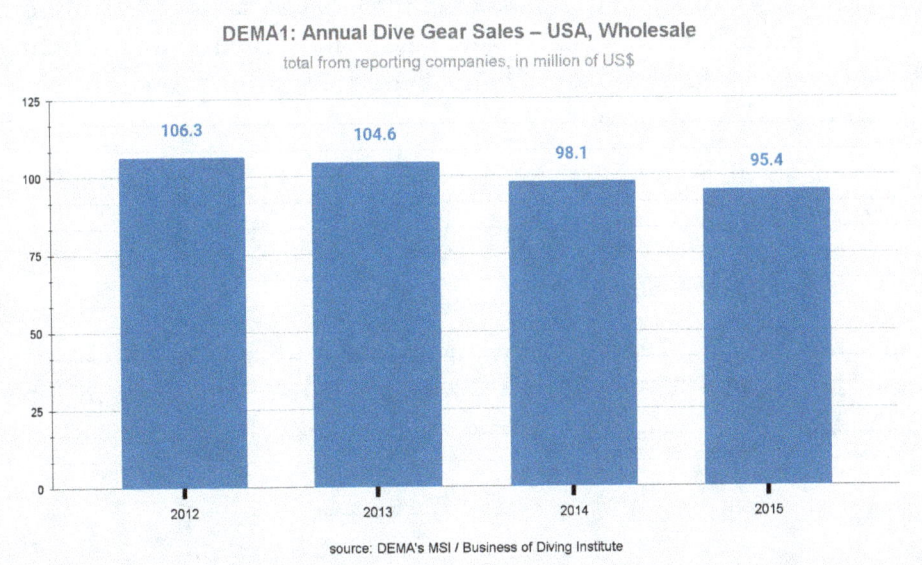

As a point of reference, the sum of dive gear sales, at wholesale pricing, reported by the following suppliers totaled about $100 million per year in the USA in 2015:

- American Underwater Products
- Aqua Lung
- Atomic Aquatics
- Innovative Scuba
- Liquivision
- Mares
- McNett
- Ocean Reef
- Scubapro
- Sherwood
- Submersible Systems (Spare Air)
- Tabata (TUSA)
- XS Scuba

When you discuss with people in the dive industry, you hear all kinds of stories. One is that Aqua Lung's sales in the USA are above $150 million. Strangely enough, the total of the dive gear brands listed above, including Aqua Lung, was $100 million. Do not believe everything you hear, especially from a dive gear rep!

That said, not all sales from these brands were reported. *They reported sales only in some categories.*

Split of Gear Revenues

The same 2015 MSI report shows us a split of dive gear sales as presented in Table DEMA2 and the components of the Scuba Units in Table DEMA3.

Table DEMA2	Leisure Trends USA 2006	TIV 2015 Germany	DEMA MSI USA 2015
Scuba Units:	27.7%	38.9%	44.4%
Fins, Masks & Snorkels:	18.6%	10.8%	24.1%
Exposure Suits:	15.2%	16.6%	10.4%
Other:	38.6%	33.6%	21.1%

Table DEMA3	Leisure Trends USA 2006	TIV 2015 Germany	DEMA MSI USA 2015
BCDs:	7.7%	8.3%	10.6%
Regulators:	9.1%	13.8%	15.5%
Computers & Gauges:	10.6%	16.9%	18.4%
Rebreathers:	0.2%	n/a	n/a
Total Scuba Units:	27.7%	38.9%	44.4%

ENTRY-LEVEL CERTIFICATIONS IN THE USA

DEMA surveys a limited number of dive training agencies (PADI, NAUI & SDI) and then extrapolates to estimate the total number of entry-level scuba diving certifications per quarter and per year in the USA. The results are presented in Figure DEMA4.

The massive drop in 2020 was obviously due to the COVID-19 pandemic. The drop in 2023 is puzzling since very other market indicator points to 2023 having been a good year for the dive industry in the USA.

ENTRY-LEVEL OPEN WATER CERTIFICATIONS BY STATE

If you operate a local dive shop in the USA, you are more interested in the size of the industry in your neck of the woods—or neck of the oceans! For you, the following Tables provide the number of entry-level open water certifications by state, as estimated by DEMA.

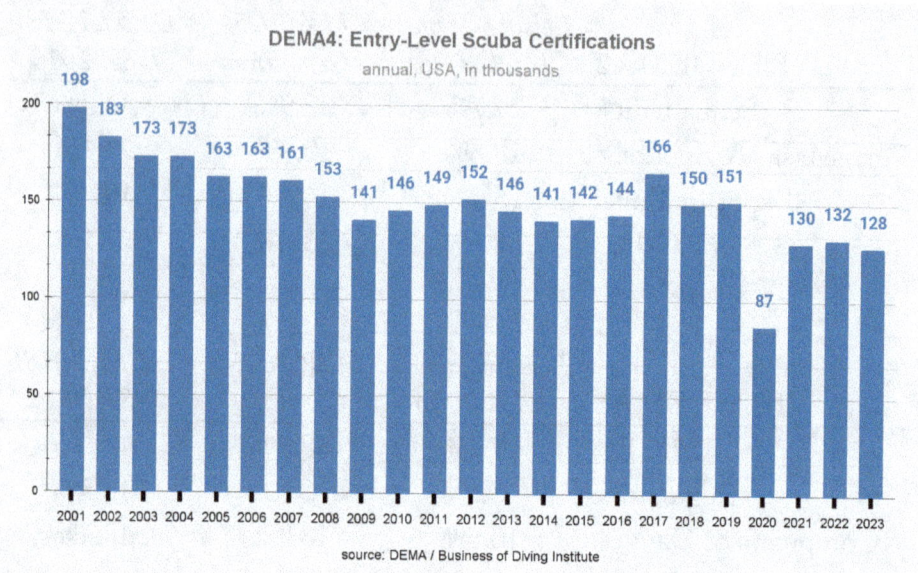

Keep in mind that a high percentage of scuba divers do their certification course while on vacation in a tropical destination. Therefore, even if a geographic region has a low level of open water certifications, you may still have a good market for selling gear and travel to scuba divers.

A better way of evaluating your market potential would be to know the participation rate by state, but this information is currently unavailable.

Please answer our dive industry market surveys at businessofdiving.com so we can eventually provide you with more market data specific to your geographic region.

Table DEMA5	Entry-level certs in 2023
California:	17,058
Washington:	4,583
Oregon:	2,055
Hawaii:	1,680
Alaska:	608
Total Pacific Region:	*25,984*

Table DEMA6	Entry-level certs in 2023
Colorado:	4,107
Arizona:	2,597
Utah:	3,394
Nevada:	1,052
Idaho:	1,315
New Mexico:	545
Montana:	553
Wyoming:	332
Total Mountain Region:	*13,895*

Table DEMA7	Entry-level certs in 2023
Virginia/Maryland/D.C.:	6,458
Georgia:	3,354
North Carolina:	4,205
South Carolina:	1,567
West Virginia:	294
Delaware:	236
Florida:	15,096
Total South Atlantic Region:	*31,210*

Table DEMA8	Entry-level certs in 2023
Illinois:	3,680
Michigan:	2,312
Ohio:	2,683
Wisconsin:	2,111
Indiana:	1,222
Total North Central Region:	*12,008*

Table DEMA9	Entry-level certs in 2023
Massachusetts:	2,860
Connecticut:	1,417
New Hampshire:	673
Maine:	477
Rhode Island:	409
Vermont:	353
Total New England Region:	*6,189*

Table DEMA10	Entry-level certs in 2023
Texas:	9,829
Oklahoma:	1,239
Arkansas:	721
Louisiana:	1,089
Total South Central Region:	*12,878*

Table DEMA11	Entry-level certs in 2023
New York:	6,756
Pennsylvania:	3,209
New Jersey:	2,681
Total Middle Atlantic Region:	*12,646*

Table DEMA12	Entry-level certs in 2023
Tennessee:	2,028
Alabama:	1,190
Kentucky:	881
Mississippi:	409
Total East South Central Region:	*4,508*

Table DEMA13	Entry-level certs in 2023
Missouri:	1,974
Minnesota:	2,368
Kansas:	791
Iowa:	613
Nebraska:	354
South Dakota:	228
North Dakota:	186
Total West North Central Region:	*6,514*

Table DEMA14	Entry-level certs in 2023
Military:	1,168
Guam/American Samoa:	657
Puerto Rico:	357
Virgin Islands:	162
Unknown:	77
Total Other Regions:	*2,421*

CERTIFICATION PER CAPITA BY STATE

In Table DEMA15, we ranked U.S. states by the number of entry-level open water certifications per capita in 2022.

As a reference point for how "outdoorsy" each state's residents are, we compared certs per capita to each state's outdoor recreation value-added as a percent of the state GDP in 2022, as we have already reviewed in a prior chapter.

Table DEMA15	Number of Entry-Level Certs per Million of Citizens	Outdoor Recreation Value Added as a % of the State GDP in 2022
U.S. Virgin Islands:	2,203	n/a
Hawaii:	1,283	5.6%
Utah:	1,180	3.2%
Colorado:	729	2.8%
Florida:	715	3.6%
Alaska:	697	4.0%
Idaho:	651	3.1%
Washington:	570	2.7%
Montana:	541	4.3%
Wyoming:	520	4.1%
Vermont:	495	4.6%
Oregon:	469	2.5%
New Hampshire:	467	3.2%
California:	463	2.0%
Minnesota:	429	2.6%
Maine:	424	3.9%
Virginia/Maryland/DC:	414	1.7%/1.7%/0.9%
Massachusetts:	392	1.7%
North Carolina:	383	2.0%
Connecticut:	379	1.4%
Arizona:	363	2.5%
New York:	340	1.5%
Texas:	336	2.0%
Rhode Island:	331	2.3%
Missouri:	329	2.2%
Nevada:	325	2.7%
Wisconsin:	322	2.5%
Kansas:	320	1.9%

Table DEMA15	Number of Entry-Level Certs per Million of Citizens	Outdoor Recreation Value Added as a % of the State GDP in 2022
Oklahoma:	319	1.9%
Georgia:	316	2.1%
South Carolina:	302	2.6%
Illinois:	294	2.1%
Tennessee:	285	2.4%
New Jersey:	284	1.7%
South Dakota:	277	2.5%
New Mexico:	270	1.9%
Arkansas:	269	2.5%
Pennsylvania:	245	1.8%
Louisiana:	241	2.7%
Michigan:	231	2.0%
Alabama:	229	2.0%
Ohio:	229	2.1%
North Dakota:	219	1.8%
Delaware:	209	1.5%
Kentucky:	192	2.0%
West Virginia:	183	1.7%
Indiana:	182	3.4%
Iowa:	179	1.9%
Nebraska:	174	1.7%
Mississippi:	130	2.4%
Puerto Rico:	121	n/a

Although these numbers indicate the number of entry-level open water certifications per capita (per million of citizens), it does not mean that these certifications were done for residents of that state.

Once again, remember that a high percentage of scuba divers do their certification course while on vacation in a tropical destination. Therefore, even if a geographic region has a low level of open water certifications, there may still be a good number of active divers.

And vice versa, in a state like Hawaii, a good percentage of the open water certifications are done to tourists visiting from out of state and out of the country.

More Data Points: USA / California / Florida

Here are some additional data points provided by DEMA. But be careful! DEMA doesn't list the source of this information nor what it includes. We must keep in mind that DEMA tends to overstate numbers to increase its relevance when lobbying governmental entities.

USA

DEMA claims that recreational scuba diving and snorkeling contribute about $11 billion to the U.S. gross domestic product (GDP) but does not indicate what is included in such a number.

California

- Annually some 1.38 million dives are made in California.
- Annual direct expenditures from scuba diving in California range from $161 million to $323 million.
- Californians and visitors account for about 3.82 million snorkeling days annually, with an estimated annual expenditure of between $170 million and $382 million.
- Estimates for expenditures in the Channel Islands National Marine Sanctuary alone range from $76 per day for divers using private vessels to $225 per day per diver for those using commercial vessels.

This is another example of the lack of reliable data. Our dive industry trade association (DEMA) estimated expenditures from snorkeling and scuba diving in California between $331M and $705M. That is a huge range!

DEMA doesn't provide its source of info. Still, it probably was quoted from "Understanding the Potential Economic Impact of Scuba Diving and Snorkeling: California" by Linwood H. Pendleton, University of California, Los Angeles, 2006.

FLORIDA

- Coral reefs in the Caribbean, including Florida, generate about $2.1 billion in revenue each year.
- Snorkeling in Florida accounts for about 4.24 million visitor days per year.
- Scuba diving in Florida accounts for about 4.56 million visitor days per year.
- Scuba diving and snorkeling create about 26,000 full-time equivalent tourism-related jobs annually in Florida.
- Visitors participating in recreational scuba diving and snorkeling contribute about $900 million to the Florida economy each year.
- In 2009, residents learning to dive in Florida contributed about $20 million in additional sales of equipment, education, and travel to the local economies.

DEMA further states that while much of Florida has natural reefs, artificial reefs also contribute to the local economy. For example, estimates from a research paper submitted by The University of West Florida indicate there are more than 4,200 chartered dive trips taken to the artificial reef of the aircraft carrier Oriskany off of Pensacola, Florida, annually, carrying divers from all over the world. Annual revenue generated from visitors traveling from Escambia and Baldwin, Florida counties alone is estimated at $2.2 million. And dive-related expenditures drive an economic impact of $3.6 million in local output and additional jobs while generating $1.4 million in local income.

DEMA does not list its sources, but the data probably partially came from "Socioeconomic Study of Reefs in Southeast Florida" by Grace M. Johns & al., 2001.

15: PADI Professional Association of Diving Instructors

PADI stands for Professional Association of Diving Instructors, although it is not an association. It is a private company that sells dive training materials and services to clients, although PADI likes to call them "members" as a marketing technique.

PADI used to provide a fair amount of valuable statistics, but in recent years, it has only released a handful of useless statistics for public relations purposes.

In 2024 press releases, PADI states:

- They have issued more than 29 million certifications since 1967.

This number includes all levels of courses, so it doesn't tell us much about the important one: new entry-level certifications.

- PADI used to claim to issue 1 million certifications (at all levels) annually, but they no longer claim it in their latest press releases.

They started listing "more than 28M certs" in 2021, up from 27 million two years earlier. In 2024, they are stating "more than 29M." This would mean an increase of 2M over four years, which, of course, includes the pandemic years.

- In 2024, PADI claims there are more than 128,000 PADI professionals worldwide, including divemasters and instructors.

This is a decrease of 5.7% from 2012 (136K) and a drop of 6.5% from 2018 (137K in 2018). Since there are more divemasters than instructors, we can only estimate that there are less than 60K PADI instructors in the world.

- PADI claims there are 6,600 PADI dive centers, an increase of 6.6% from 2012 (6191) and the same level since 2018 (6,600).

For more information (or lack thereof): www.padi.com

Otherwise, in 1995, PADI published a book, "The Business of Diving," that contained information on the size of the dive industry around the world. It was last updated in 2008.

Retail Sales – USA

In the 2008 "Business of Diving" book, PADI quotes a 1994 DEMA report with the following figures for U.S. retail sales in the dive industry:

- Dive gear & training: $1 billion
- Travel: $1.6 billion

These numbers are old—we know! But the dive industry hasn't experienced sky-rocketing growth. Quite the contrary! Yet, the decline has been gradual. Therefore, they can still serve as historical data points.

Retail Sales – Outside the USA

In this 2008 book, PADI estimates the following dive markets (in millions of US$):

- Germany: $20M
- Italy: $20M
- France: $15M
- Switzerland: $5 to 6M
- Austria: $3 to 4M

This makes no sense. It would indicate that the European market would be less than 10% of the American market.

From the dive industry association in Germany (TIV), we know that dive gear sales in Germany alone exceed €80M ($87M). Therefore, the entire German dive industry can not be $20 million. There is something utterly absurd in these numbers. Moving right along!

Number of Dive Centers – Worldwide

In the same 2008 book, PADI estimates the number of dive centers around the world at:

- USA: 1,700 to 2,200
- Japan: 1,540
- Australia: 320

- Switzerland: 70

Worldwide, PADI states that there are approximately 4,000 to 4,500 dive centers, of which 55 to 60% are PADI.

Well, the sum of the four countries listed above already gets us close to 4,000! Furthermore, in its corporate statistics, PADI stated there were 5,861 PADI dive centers in the world in 2008 and 4,642 in 1999. So, how can they get to an overall estimate of 4,000 dive centers worldwide in 2008?

PADI's statistics must be the least reliable ones we have reviewed so far!

16: Centre for Conservation Geography – Australia

We get valuable Australian dive industry numbers from a March 2015 report by the Centre for Conservation Geography: "The Scuba Dive Industry in Australia: Towards estimates of economic size and impact."

Dive-related spending in Australia is presented in Table AU1.

Table AU1	Share	Dive Spending in million of AU$
New South Wales:	23%	513
Queensland:	43%	951
Western Australia:	20%	446
Other:	13%	289
Total:	100%	2,199

The AU$2.2 billion (US$1.4B) in spending is estimated to come from:

- 1.7B from tourists (77%)
- 0.5B from Australians (23%)

These numbers capture much more than what is actually spent in the "dive industry" per se. It includes hotels, transportation, and all kinds of expenditures that are not incurred in dive businesses.

In people participating in scuba diving, they estimate:

- 280K international visitors
- 185K Australians

For more information: conservationgeography.org

17: Rebreather Forum

The following market data about the state of rebreather diving was shared at Rebreather Forum 4 in Malta in 2023.

Rebreather Diving Certifications

The following certification statistics resulted from a census conducted by a third party using data from BSAC, GUE, SDI, TDI, FFESSM, SSI, PADI, IANTD, and RAID.

The number of certifications includes basic, intermediate and advanced courses. Therefore, it does not indicate the number of active rebreather divers since double counting exists.

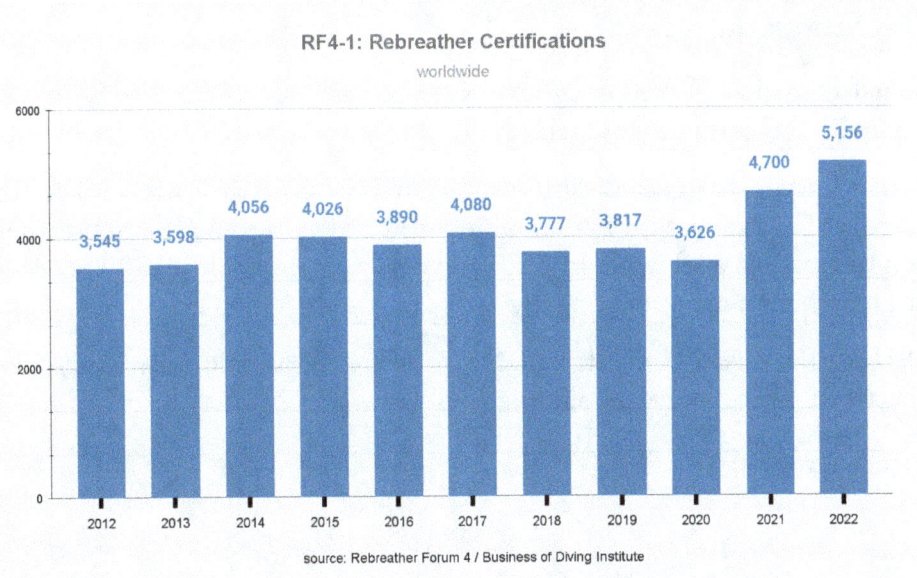

Rebreather Diving Certifications by Geographic Market

The same data set indicates that rebreather diving is much more prevalent in Europe than anywhere else in the world, as we can see on Figure RF4-2.

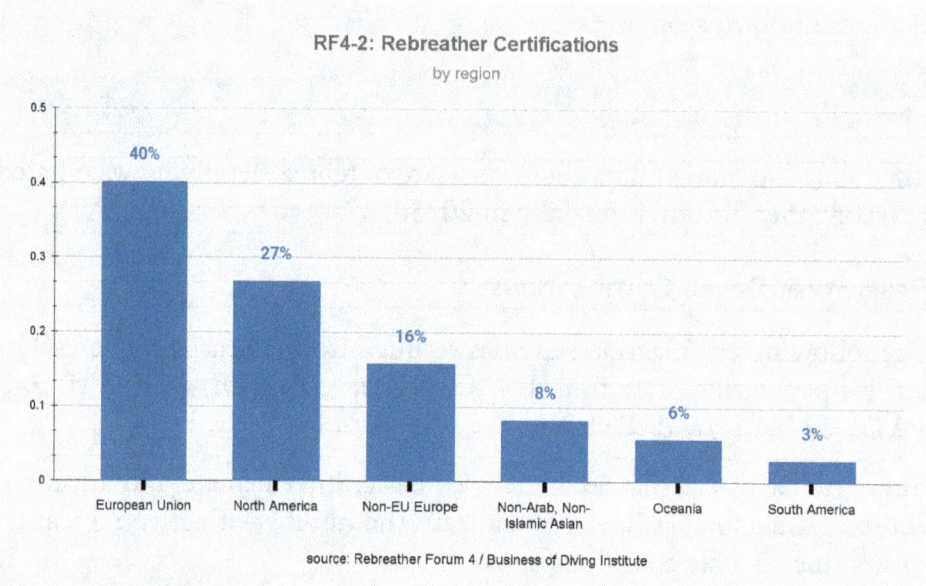

source: Rebreather Forum 4 / Business of Diving Institute

Rebreather Units Sold

For Rebreather Forum 4, DAN conducted an industry survey with data from 20 rebreather manufacturers.

Their findings suggested significant growth in the rebreather market over the last few years, with a total of between 25,000 and 35,000 rebreathers on the market worldwide in 2023 and between 1,400 and 2,800 new certified rebreather divers annually.

Rebreather divers were estimated to be 84% to 95% male, with a mean age between 42 and 46 years old.

Section 3: Business of Diving Institute Surveys & Studies

The Business of Diving Institute (BODI) provides dive industry market studies and strategic analysis through its publication Scubanomics.com and consulting services to dive industry investors and professionals.

Because of a severe lack of reliable market data in the dive industry, the Business of Diving Institute has increased the number of market surveys it conducts. We're sharing here survey results related to evaluating the size of the dive industry.

Please participate in our ongoing surveys so that the next edition of this report can be even more valuable to you.

For more information: www.businessofdiving.com

18: Scuba Try-outs / Discover Scuba Diving

In 2021, we paid to survey a random sample of the American population to get statistically valid market information.

It gave us surprising results:

- 32.7% of the American population had tried scuba diving in one way or another in their life.

This can be in any way, shape, or form, from a scuba try-out in a pool to a complete scuba diving certification course.

The Dropout Rate

From SFIA, we know the scuba diving participation rate among the American population is about 1% (0.98% of 6+). This means that only 3% of American adults who had tried scuba diving were still active divers. We lost 97% of them!

The dropout rate is a touchy discussion in the dive industry.

Usually, the dropout rate is estimated based on how many fully certified divers have stopped diving. In reality, we may want to assess the dropout rate based on how many people have tried scuba diving and never did it afterward. After all, "Discover Scuba Diving" is often presented to dive professionals as a way to recruit clients for scuba diving certification classes, and it is a big part of many dive resort revenues.

However, we need to do more research to determine the actual dropout rate.

Number of Scuba Tryouts in The World

In 2013, a PADI representative estimated that about 1 million official "Discover Scuba Diving" experiences were conducted annually worldwide, plus at least another 5 million non-reported ones. That's a total of at least 6 million scuba tryouts per year.

PADI also estimated that about 250 thousand official Discover Scuba Diving (DSD) experiences had been completed in the USA in 2008—which is 1.6 times the number of entry-level certifications issued in the USA in that year (153K). At a ratio of 5 non-official DSD to 1 officially reported DSD, it would mean 1.5 million Americans experienced a scuba tryout that year.

If you add those DSDs to the number of entry-level certifications over the course of 50 years, you quickly reach 32.7% from our survey of the U.S. population.

The Size of The Scuba Tryout Market

We often see the dive industry size estimated based on the number of new certifications and the number of active divers. It somehow makes sense because we have estimates on how much a new diver spends and how much a core or casual, active diver spends per year.

Yet, scuba tryouts end up being excluded from such estimates while it is a massive market of its own.

A scuba tryout is often sold for more than $100 to tourists around the world. At 6 million scuba tryouts per year, we have a market of $600 million right there.

These people rarely buy gear, though, and the trip expenses were not for a dive trip. But that $600 million is part of the dive training market size because it is provided by scuba diving instructors if the dive operator respects industry standards.

19: How Much Scuba Divers Spend Annually on Dive Gear, Travel, Training & Services

In 2023, we conducted an extensive scuba diving industry market survey on how much scuba divers spend annually on dive gear, travel, training, and services. It was part of our goal to collect market data from many different angles to better evaluate the size of the scuba diving industry.

We looked at how results compared between:

- core vs. casual divers
- recreational vs. tech divers
- European vs. American divers

Unfortunately, we did not get enough answers outside of Western Europe and the USA to provide results in other markets. Please help us recruit divers and dive professionals around the world to participate in our surveys so we can provide you with more precise market data.

Thanks to the SFIA, we have a very good estimate of the number of active divers in the USA. Therefore, we specifically looked at spending amounts by core and casual divers in the USA to estimate the size of the U.S. market. Later, we hope to be able to do the same for all markets.

Who Answered The Survey?

A total of 525 scuba divers participated in the survey.

Age groups (generations) of scuba divers who answered the survey:

- Boomers I (1946–1954): 2.9%
- Boomers II/Generation Jones (1955–1964): 10.1%
- Gen X (1965–1980): 44.9%
- Millennials (1981–1996): 36.2%
- Gen Z (1997–2012): 5.8%

The geographic region of residence:

- U.S.A.: 33.3%
- Western Europe: 34.8%
- Mexico, Central America, Caribbean, Tropical Atlantic: 8.7%
- South Pacific, Indo-Pacific, Other Tropical Asia-Pacific Region (incl. Maldives): 7.25%
- Australia & New Zealand: 5.8%
- All other regions had less than 5% of the survey respondents.

Gender:

- Male: 82.6%
- Female: 13.0%
- Other/Non-binary/Prefer Not To Say: 4.4%

Core vs. Casual Divers:

To be able to compare results with those provided by the SFIA (Sports & Fitness Industry Association) in the USA, we used the same definitions as the SFIA:

- **Core Diver**: A scuba diver who has gone scuba diving 8 or more times in the prior 12 months
- **Casual Diver**: A scuba diver who has gone diving less than 8 times in the prior 12 months (but at least once)

As is the case with all dive industry surveys, we got more participation from avid scuba divers, with 60.5% of respondents fitting the definition of core divers, while they were only 22% of the market in 2023.

It has always been difficult for all organizations to get survey participation from casual divers.

Newly Certified Scuba Divers:

4.8% of survey respondents had obtained their entry-level open-water certification in the prior 12 months.

Tech Divers:

62.9% of survey respondents were tech divers.

In this survey, tech divers were over-represented compared to recreational (non-tech) divers. It is explained by the fact that tech divers are typically more involved in scuba diving (more likely to be core divers) and because the Business of Diving Institute administered this scuba diving industry market survey in collaboration with InDEPTH Magazine, which specializes in tech diving.

Currency:

We converted all answers to U.S. dollars, although respondents could answer in their own currencies. Numerous online tools for currency conversion are available if you want to convert the figures back to your own currency. At the time of writing this market report, one U.S. dollar equals 0.92 Euros.

How Much Scuba Divers Spend Annually on Training

- Tech Divers: $443
- Recreational (Non-Tech) Divers: $119
- European Divers: $181
- American Divers: $133
- Casual Divers USA: $124
- Core Divers USA: $164

With 2.37 million casual divers and 689K core divers in the USA (source: SFIA, 2023), the scuba diving training market in the USA would be about $400 million annually. However, if we adjust for an over-representation of tech divers who spend more, we get to less than $300 million.

Percentage of Scuba Courses Done Locally

On average, survey respondents spent 55% of their training expenses locally and paid the rest in dive destinations requiring travel. Because core divers tend to be more involved with their local dive shop, the actual percentage must be estimated to be lower than 50%.

How Much Scuba Divers Spend Annually on Dive Gear

- Tech Divers: $970
- Recreational (Non-Tech) Divers: $252
- European Divers: $361
- American Divers: $281
- Casual Divers USA: $132
- Core Divers USA: $747

With 2.374 million casual divers and 689K core divers in the USA in 2023 (source: SFIA), the scuba diving equipment market in the USA would be around $800 million annually. However, we must factor in that an over-representation of tech divers in this survey pushes these figures up, especially in the core diver segment. With adjustment for tech divers, we get to a market of less than $700 million.

It is no surprise that core divers spend more on dive gear. Unfortunately, the number of core divers is shrinking, while new divers tend to be casual ones.

Based on these results, 3.9% of active scuba divers in the USA would be tech divers.

How Much Scuba Divers Spend Annually on Used Dive Gear

On average, scuba divers who answered our survey spent annually $98 buying second-hand diver gear.

Based on these survey results, the second-hand market is about 40% of the market for new dive gear. Assuming that second-hand gear is sold on average at 50% of the retail price of new dive gear, it would mean that more than half of new dive gear is eventually resold on the second-hand market. This is much more than we expected and will require further study.

WHERE SCUBA DIVERS BUY THEIR DIVE GEAR

- Online From The Gear Manufacturer/Brand: 25.9%
- Online From Other Sources: 27.5%
- In a Physical Store: Dive-Specialized Retailer (e.g., a local dive shop): 42.7%
- In a Physical Store: Non-Dive-Specialized Retailer (e.g., Decathlon, West Marine): 3.8%

Based on these survey results, more dive gear is now sold online than in physical stores.

However, a survey of dive gear manufacturers that we conducted in 2024 found that about 40% of dive gear is sold online in the USA and 50% in Western Europe. We will review this survey in the next chapter.

SPLIT OF DIVE GEAR PURCHASES BY CATEGORY OF PRODUCT

The percentage each dive gear category holds in the total dive gear market, based on the results of this survey, is in parenthesis.

- Fins, Masks & Snorkels: $17.86 (5.9%)
- Exposure Protection, including Wetsuits, Skins, Drysuits, Booties, Socks, Gloves & Hoods: $76.11 (25.0%)
- BC-related Hard Goods, including BCDs, Harnesses, Wings, Bladders & Back Plates: $43.34 (14.3%)
- Scuba Diving-enabled Smart Watches (e.g., Apple Ultra, Huawei Ultimate): $11.56 (3.8%)
- Other Dive Computers, including Wrist-mount & Console-integrated: $52.40 (17.2%)
- Analog Instruments, including Depth Gauge, SPG & Compass: $8.17 (2.7%)

- Regulator-related Hard Goods, including Regulators 1st & 2nd Stages, Octopus (excluding instruments): $38.97 (12.8%)
- Cylinders: $26.69 (8.8%)
- Paper Logbooks: $0.94 (0.3%)
- Accessories, including Bags, Weights, Anti-fog, Dive Flags, Reels, Slates, Mouthpieces, Fin Straps, etc.: $27.97 (9.2%)

Table BODI1	*TIV 2015 Germany*	*DEMA MSI USA 2015*	*BODI 2023*
Scuba Units:	38.9%	44.4%	50.8%
Fins, Masks & Snorkels:	10.8%	24.1%	5.9%
Exposure Suits:	16.6%	10.4%	25.0%
Other:	33.6%	21.1%	18.3%

Table BODI2	*TIV 2015 Germany*	*DEMA MSI USA 2015*	*BODI 2023*
BCDs:	8.3%	10.6%	14.3%
Regulators:	13.8%	15.5%	12.8%
Computers & Gauges:	16.9%	18.4%	23.7%
Total Scuba Units:	38.9%	44.4%	50.8%

Although there seems to be an incongruity between the 2015 data sets and the results of our 2023 market survey, the way the data was collected can explain it.

When DEMA surveyed dive gear manufacturers, they collected data on all dive gear sales, including snorkeling equipment. Meanwhile, our 2023 survey was conducted only with scuba divers. Snorkelers were not part of our 2023 survey respondents, which explains the much lower sales of fins, masks, and snorkels in the percentage of all dive gear sold.

Otherwise, the unusually high figure for computers is likely a result of an overrepresentation of tech divers among our survey respondents. All tech divers use at least one dive computer, and these tend to be more expensive units than the ones used by recreational divers.

How Much Rebreather Divers Spend Annually on Rebreathers & Rebreather Supplies

Rebreather divers have spent an annual average of:

- $983 on purchasing rebreathers
- $791 on consumables related to rebreather diving (sorb, O2 cells, etc.), excluding fills
- $811 on fills (air, nitrox, trimix, or any other kind)

How Much Scuba Divers Spend Annually on Renting Dive Gear

- Casual Divers: $59
- Core Divers: $55

How Much Scuba Divers Spend Annually on Servicing Their Dive Gear

- Casual Divers: $24
- Core Divers: $148

How Much Scuba Divers Spend Annually on Cylinder Fills

This is the amount scuba divers paid separately for fills, and therefore, it excludes fills that were included in a package like an all-inclusive dive resort vacation or a dive course.

- Casual Divers: $0.52
- Core Divers: $249

It appears casual divers typically do not pay for fills, as cylinders and fills are usually included in dive travel packages.

How Much Scuba Divers Spend Annually on Dive Outings & Dive Travel

Here are the definitions we used in this survey.

- A "**dive outing**" is usually done at a dive site that you can reach by car and from which you can return home without requiring a night stay.
- A "**dive trip**" involves diving at a destination where you will spend one or more nights. It usually involves a flight, but not necessarily. For instance, a New York scuba diver could drive to Key Largo, and a Melbourne diver could go to Cairns for a diving vacation week.

Casual Divers:

- Dive Outings (without transportation): $10
- Dive Trips (without transportation but with accommodations): $1,386
- Transportation (Airfare) for Dive Trips: $334

Core Divers:

- Dive Outings (without transportation): $690
- Dive Trips (without transportation but with accommodations): $2,980
- Transportation (Airfare) for Dive Trips: $1,640

It appears that casual divers do not participate much in local diving (dive outings).

Scuba Divers Who Also Participate in Freediving & Snorkeling

Percentage of active scuba divers who answered our survey and also active in the following activities:

- Freediving: 23%
- Snorkeling: 68%

20: Dive Gear Manufacturers Sales Channels & Online Sales

In 2023, we started conducting an annual State of the Industry (SOTI) market survey of the dive industry.

Part of that survey involved dive gear manufacturers indicating the percentage of gear they sell through their various sales channels.

Table SOTI1	2022	2023
Direct-to-Customer (online):	14%	26%
Independent Dive Professionals:	3%	5%
Dive-Specialized Retailers:	66%	51%
Non-Dive-Specialized Retailers:	17%	18%

We have to be careful when factoring in these numbers in our evaluation of the size of the dive gear market because revenues from direct-to-consumer are at retail prices while sales to dive-specialized shops are at wholesale. Furthermore, we evaluate that about half the sales in the "dive-specialized retailers" category are to traditional brick-and-mortar local dive shops and the other half to non-traditional specialized retailers.

Meanwhile, in the same survey, traditional dive retailers provided the percentage of their sales done online.

Table SOTI2	USA 2023	Western Europe 2023
Online Gear Sales:	9%	29%
Online Training Sales:	28%	41%

If we mix these two sets of results with an estimate of how much non-traditional specialized retailers sell online, we get to a percentage of dive gear sold online of approximately 39% in the USA and 48% in Western Europe.

21: Benchmarking Local Dive Shops in Western Europe & USA

Dive centers worldwide participated in our State of the Industry (SOTI) survey of the dive industry.

We can only provide statistics on local scuba diving centers in the USA and Western Europe because we did not get enough participation in other geographical regions to provide statistically valid results. We need your help!

Participating in our surveys and inviting your colleagues to do so can help us provide you with better dive industry market reports

The following results are for dive centers in origin markets, excluding dive resorts which we cover in the next chapter.

Number of Employees per Scuba Diving Center

Table SOTI3	USA 2022	USA 2023
Regular Full-Time:	3.1	4.2
Regular Part-Time:	2.2	3.8
Occasional/Seasonal:	1.7	1.8

Table SOTI4	Western Europe 2022	Western Europe 2023
Regular Full-Time:	2.1	2.1
Regular Part-Time:	1.8	2.8
Occasional/Seasonal:	3.0	3.0

On average, local dive shops in the USA employ more regular full-time staff, while dive shops in Western Europe rely more on occasional or seasonal employees.

During the pandemic, many dive centers went out of business, and new openings have not offset that loss. It appears that the dive centers still in business may be, on average, larger dive operations based on the number of employees.

NUMBER OF DIVEMASTER & DIVE INSTRUCTORS PER SCUBA DIVING CENTER

Table SOTI5	USA 2023	Western Europe 2023
Divemasters or equivalent:	3.9	1.2
Instructors:	8.5	3.8
Instructor Trainers:	1.4	0.9

AVERAGE ANNUAL DIVE SHOP REVENUES

Table SOTI6	USA 2023	Western Europe 2023
Annual Sales (US$):	$541,200	$439,771

Keep in mind that it is typically the best dive centers and dive professionals who answer dive industry surveys, and therefore, results tend to be skewed toward the more positive or larger size.

PERCENTAGE OF DIVE CENTER REVENUES BY DEPARTMENT

Table SOTI7	USA 2023	Western Europe 2023
Training:	32%	37%
Gear Sales:	27%	28%
Renting Gear:	7%	6%
Repair & Maintenance:	9%	9%
Fill Station:	5%	5%
Day-Trips:	6%	11%
Travel:	14%	5%

Selling dive gear is becoming relatively less significant for dive centers, while "diving" is becoming more important as we can in the evolution in the USA from 2006 to 2023.

Table SOTI8	LT 2006	SOTI 2023
Equipment:	54.8%	27%
Training:	20.0%	32%
Local Dive Outings:	8.7%	6%
Repair & Maintenance:	7.9%	9%
Renting Gear:	5.7%	7%
Other:	2.9%	19%

AVERAGE SALES OF DIVE GEAR PER NEW STUDENT-DIVER

Table SOTI9	USA 2022	USA 2023
Gear Sales per Entry-Level Student (US$):	$494	$427

Table SOTI10	Western Europe 2022	Western Europe 2023
Gear Sales per Entry-Level Student (US$):	$650	$611

The decrease in average dive gear purchased by new open-water student divers is consistent with a higher percentage of casual divers.

PRODUCT-MIX IN LOCAL DIVE SHOPS

From our 2023 state of the dive industry survey, these are the percentage of dive centers offering the following products and services.

21: BENCHMARKING LOCAL DIVE SHOPS IN WESTERN EUROPE & USA

Table SOTI11	USA 2023	Western Europe 2023
Recreational Dive Gear:	98%	88%
Swim Gear & Accessories:	48%	45%
Snorkeling Equipment:	91%	55%
Freediving Equipment:	48%	51%
Surface-Supplied Air Diving Eq.:	9%	10%
Rebreathers:	22%	57%
Sidemount Diving Equipment:	57%	55%
Other Tech Diving Gear:	43%	45%
Surf Boards & Accessories:	0%	8%
Paddleboards & Accessories:	13%	19%
Apparel:	22%	9%
Air Fills:	96%	86%
Nitrox Fills up to 40%:	78%	73%
Nitrox Fills above 40%:	48%	71%
Trimix/Heliox Fills:	30%	64%
Day-Trips:	39%	18%
Travel:	78%	19%

Traditionally, freediving was a much more significant source of revenue for dive shops in Europe than in the USA. However, we've witnessed an increase in the percentage of American dive shops carrying freediving equipment over the past few years.

Selling snorkeling equipment remains more significant in the USA than in Western Europe.

Rebreathers are more widely available in European dive centers, which is consistent with the data shared at Rebreather Forum 4.

Meanwhile, fly-away scuba diving vacations are more readily offered in American dive shops.

22: BENCHMARKING DIVE RESORTS

2024 was the first year we got enough participation from dive resorts in our state of the dive industry survey to report on them. However, the sample size remained too small to do a geographic segmentation.

We need your help! Participating in our surveys and inviting your scuba divers and dive professionals to do so can help us provide you with better dive industry market reports

The following results are for dive resorts in tourist destinations. In the previous chapter, we reviewed dive centers in origin markets.

79% of respondents in the dive resort category were business owners or co-owners, while 21% were managers. They all worked full-time in the dive resort.

Survey respondents operated dive resorts in the following regions:

- 56% South Pacific, Indo-Pacific & Other Tropical Asia-Pacific Region
- 37% Mexico, Central America, Caribbean & Tropical Atlantic
- 7% Western Europe

PRODUCTS & SERVICES OFFERED IN DIVE RESORTS

Here are the percentage of dive resorts offering the following products and services.

Table SOTI12	2023
Snorkeling:	61%
Freediving:	24%
Try Scuba:	100%
Recreational Scuba Diving:	100%
Sidemount Diving:	63%
Rebreather Diving:	18%
Other Tech Diving:	45%
Surface-Supplied Air Diving/SNUBA:	0%

22: BENCHMARKING DIVE RESORTS

Table SOTI12	2023
Disabled/Handicapped Scuba Diving:	0%
Dive Gear Sales:	51%
Gear Rental or Loan:	100%
Dive Gear Repair & Maintenance:	36%
Air Fills:	100%
Nitrox Fills up to 40%:	100%
Nitrox Fills above 40%:	44%
Trimix/Heliox Fills:	14%

PERCENTAGE OF DIVE RESORTS' BOOKINGS BY SALES CHANNEL

Table SOTI13	2023
Direct-to-Consumer Individuals:	51%
Direct-to-Consumer Groups:	16%
Groups by Independent Dive Pros:	4%
Dive Centers:	9%
Travel Wholesalers:	6%
Travel Agencies/Agents:	15%

COMMISSIONS PAID BY DIVE RESORTS

Table SOTI14	2023
Direct-to-Consumer Groups:	16%
Groups by Independent Dive Pros:	21%
Dive Centers:	20%
Travel Wholesalers:	30%
Travel Agencies/Agents:	24%

Number of Employees per Dive Resort

	Table SOTI15	2023
	Regular Full-Time:	26.4
	Regular Part-Time:	4.6
	Occasional/Seasonal:	2.4

Number of Divemaster & Dive Instructors per Dive Resort

	Table SOTI16	2023
	Divemasters or equivalent:	4.9
	Instructors:	7.3
	Instructor Trainers:	0.8

23: The Size of the Dive Industry

We used all of the numbers reviewed so far in this book, considered the population size and geographic location of all regions for which we have data, and ran some extrapolation and correlation to arrive at a verdict on the size of the dive industry, as presented in Table SUM.

The markets outside of the USA and Europe, which are presented as "the rest of the world," are much more significant regarding training and travel expenses because many scuba diving Americans and Europeans spend most of their training and travel money outside of Europe and the USA. Scuba diving is mainly a tropical activity, even if there is some "local diving."

It is important to note that Europe's population is 2.3 times larger than the USA's. Therefore, even with a similar level of spending, the USA remains the most significant market per capita for dive gear.

Tropical dive destinations typically do not sell much dive gear but purchase a fair amount of rental dive gear for tourists.

"Trips" refer to day trips, while "travel" refers to fly-away adventures requiring an overnight stay.

"Other" includes repair & maintenance, rental revenues, and fill station fees.

Please do not compare results from the first edition to the following conclusions to infer growth or decline in the dive industry. Changes between the two editions mainly relate to having access to additional market data, especially dive industry surveys by the Business of Diving Institute.

SCUBA DIVING INDUSTRY MARKET SIZE RESEARCH REPORTS (2ND EDITION)

Table SUM

All $ values are at retail prices. M = Million

2024	Number of Active Divers	Gear Sales	Training including Scuba Tryouts	Trips & Travel	Other	Total
USA	3.0M	$690M	$247M	$1,995M	$156M	$3,088M
Europe	2.8M	$655M	$234M	$1,889M	$147M	$2,925M
Rest of the World	2.8M	$650M	$1,443M	$9,323M	$146M	$11,562M
Total	8.6M	$1,995M	$1,924M	$13,207M	$449M	$17,575M

source: businessofdiving.com

Section 4: What's Next?

24: How To Accurately Measure The Size of The Dive Industry

Besides the fact that dive gear manufacturers and dive training agencies tend to be paranoid and generally refuse to collaborate on initiatives to establish systematic dive industry measures, we face the reality that *surveying dive gear manufacturers and dive training agencies could never give us a complete picture of the market anyway*, even if they shared data with a third party tasked with providing market reports.

In the first section of this book, we discussed the numerous reasons why such a set of numbers would come with gigantic holes. For many other reasons, *surveying dive retailers also provides an incomplete picture of the industry.*

There are simply too many stakeholders in a wide variety of types of businesses to be able to rely on stakeholder surveys to measure the dive industry in numerous geographic markets.

These surveys can give us an indication of the size of the dive industry and how it is growing or shrinking. The Business of Diving Institute is regularly involved in administering that type of survey, and the results helped us with the conclusions we reached in this book.

However, if we want a truly accurate picture of the dive industry, we will need to conduct surveys directly with end-users.

The most reliable data we currently have comes from the SFIA because they use a specialized firm to *randomly* contact Americans to establish participation rates in various sports and fitness activities. The TIV in Germany used a similar process to get the numbers we reviewed in a prior chapter.

We simply need to dig further than what is probed in the annual SFIA participation surveys.

We could establish a list of questions to segment respondents into categories for which we expect spending to be at different levels, like:

- Scuba divers & dive professionals
- Casual divers & core divers
- Tech divers & recreational divers

Then, we simply need to ask them how much they have spent on dive gear, dive training, dive travel, and other dive services in the prior 12 months.

This would give us a complete and accurate portrayal of the dive industry.

By doing such a survey, we could also know how much divers spend locally compared to what they spend at remote locations when they travel.

Such a survey would have numerous other advantages, like being able to determine the dropout rate once and for all by simply querying who went scuba diving at one point in their lives compared to active scuba divers who have gone underwater in the prior 12 months.

And we could run such a survey in any geographic region.

Of course, an issue with this solution is the cost of administering the survey. SFIA pays a subcontractor to do this. We could join the SFIA and work with them to establish these additional questions, just like OIA and other trade associations have joined SFIA in these annual market research initiatives. It would likely cost us less to contribute to the SFIA surveys than to conduct our own surveys.

But even conducting our own surveys would not be cost-prohibitive if dive industry stakeholders could recognize the value of having reliable market data and get together to collect it.

Because the participation rate in scuba diving is relatively low (about 1% in the USA, for instance), we would need to contact a large number of people to obtain an acceptable sample size. For example, if we wanted to survey 1,000 active scuba divers in the USA, we would need to contact about 100,000 Americans.

It may be a $100,000 project just to evaluate the American market, and then we would still want to assess all the other markets around the world. But if dive gear manufacturers, training agencies, dive retailers, and other stakeholders could collaborate, the cost would be relatively small for each contributor.

If you are interested in working on this project and running a test in one market, please contact me at businessofdiving.com.

In the meantime, I hope the numbers in this book will be valuable to your dive industry business planning.

Also From Darcy Kieran

If you would like volume pricing for any of our books for your instructors, instructor candidats, divemasters, divers or student-divers, please contact: publisher@businessofdiving.com.

Together, we can raise the bar!

Your CAREER and/or LIFE as a SCUBA DIVING INSTRUCTOR

Darcy Kieran
Business of Diving Institute

SPF SCUBA DIVING ADVANCED LOGBOOK & CHECKLISTS FOR CERTIFIED DIVERS, DIVEMASTERS & INSTRUCTORS

Criteria for Selecting Dive Centers, Buoyancy & Trim Mastery, Self-Debriefing & Scuba Diver Creed

ADVANCED LOGBOOK & CHECKLISTS

SAFETY ~ PERFORMANCE ~ FUN

Darcy Kieran
The Business of Diving Institute

The *Evolved* SCUBA DIVER LOGBOOK

EXTENDED EVOLUTION
What Goes Up
Must Come Down

DARCY KIERAN

A Neo-Noir Dive Into Crime, Passion, and The Abyss

MYSTERY OF THE BLUE DRAGON

Feedback, Please

First of all, thank you for purchasing or reading one of our business of diving books.

We hope to help scuba professionals and the dive industry by providing information and market data while encouraging discussions that urge us all to do better, to be better.

But we realize that sometimes, we may have pushed the "publish" button before including everything you would have expected to see and read. *If this book didn't satisfy your needs, please, let us know by filling up the form at* businessofdiving.com/feedback, and we will do our best to meet your needs. We're all in this together!

On the other hand, *if our work helped you, please leave us a review*. It would make our day! You will find shortcuts to review sites at businessofdiving.com/feedback.

We appreciate your feedback and hope to cross paths with you one day, preferably on a dive site somewhere!

Connect With Us

- All Books: businessofdiving.com/books
- Subscribe to Our eMail Newsletters: businessofdiving.com/subscribe
- Contact Us: businessofdiving.com/contact
- LinkedIn: www.linkedin.com/in/darcykieran

About Us

About The Business of Diving Institute

We're passionate about going beyond the passion for scuba diving!

The Business of Diving Institute (BODI) was created shortly after Darcy purchased his first dive center as a sideline. At the time, he was in charge of sales for the largest division of a multi-billion dollar international transport company with vast staff training resources, and he could not comprehend the lack of training programs available to his dive store and dive training staff.

Many dive certification agencies were eager to show his team how to remove and replace a mask underwater. However, nobody provided customer service training — or any other staff training — tailored to the dive industry. It is to address this problem that BODI was born.

The Business of Diving Institute and Darcy Kieran publish two online publications: Scubanomics for dive professionals and Scuba Diver Press for scuba divers, snorkelers, and tankless diving adepts.

About Darcy Kieran

"Even if you're on the right track, you'll get run over if you just sit there." ~Will Rogers

In the dive industry, Darcy has been a Course Director and Instructor Trainer with multiple dive training agencies for recreational and tech diving. He owned/managed dive shops, dive gear distributors and wholesalers, dive resorts, and charter boats in Canada and the USA.

He's been on the Board of Directors of the Diving Equipment & Marketing Association (DEMA), a dive industry trade association based in California. And he brought with him valuable experience from other industries, including sporting goods manufacturing, radio & TV broadcasting, transportation, digital marketing agencies, and education. Darcy is an engineer, radio announcer, public speaker, and author.

www.ingramcontent.com/pod-product-compliance
Lightning Source LLC
Chambersburg PA
CBHW072212070526
44585CB00015B/1306